Researching conflict in Africa

Researching conflict in Africa: Insights and experiences

Edited by Elisabeth Porter, Gillian Robinson, Marie Smyth, Albrecht Schnabel and Eghosa Osaghae

United Nations University Press

TOKYO · NEW YORK · PARIS

United Nations University Press
United Nations University, 53-70, Jingumae 5-chome,
Shibuya-ku, Tokyo, 150-8925, Japan
Tel: +81-3-3499-2811   Fax: +81-3-3406-7345
E-mail: sales@hq.unu.edu
General enquiries: press@hq.unu.edu
http://www.unu.edu

United Nations University Office at the United Nations, New York
2 United Nations Plaza, Room DC2-2062, New York, NY 10017, USA
Tel: +1-212-963-6387   Fax: +1-212-371-9454
E-mail: unuona@ony.unu.edu

United Nations University Press is the publishing division of the United Nations University.

Cover design by Mea Rhee

Printed in Hong Kong

ISBN 92-808-1119-3

Library of Congress Cataloging-in-Publication Data

Researching conflict in Africa : insights and experiences / edited by Elisabeth Porter ... [et al.].
    p.   cm.
  Includes bibliographical references and index.
  ISBN 9280811193 (pbk.)
  1. Social conflict—Research—Africa. 2. Ethnic conflict—Research—Africa.
3. Violence—Research—Africa. 4. Research—Moral and ethical aspects—Africa. I. Porter, Elisabeth J.
HN780.Z9S628   2005
303.6′072′06—dc22   2005022850

Contents

Acknowledgements

We are grateful to the following funders for their support of the Researching Divided Societies programme: The United Nations University; The Ford Foundation; The British Council; and the former Central Community Relations Unit of Government, Northern Ireland.

INCORE (International Conflict Research) at the University of Ulster is associated with the United Nations University and has worked in partnership with their Peace and Governance Programme on this research programme. We also collaborated with CEPACS (The Centre for Peace and Conflict Studies) at the University of Ibadan, Nigeria, and are particularly grateful to everyone there for their support with the African Workshop from which this book is drawn. We owe special thanks to the University of the Andes, Bogota, Colombia, for collaborating with us in two workshops held in 2003 on the special issues facing researchers in Colombia.

Finally, we acknowledge with appreciation the research assistance and typing help of INCORE interns, Mangadar Situmorang from Indonesia, Johanna Karlsson from Sweden, and Alessia Montanari from Italy.

List of abbreviations

AU	African Union
CIDA	Canadian International Development Association
DFID	Department for International Development
DRC	Democratic Republic of Congo
ECOWAS	Economic Community of West African States
ERP	Economic Recovery Programme
FGDs	focus group discussions
Profemme	*Collectif des Associations Rwandaises de Promotion de la Femme* (Collective of Rwandan Associations of Promotion of Women, Peace and Development)
GNU	Government of National Unity
IDPs	internally displaced persons
IDRC	International Research and Development Centre
IGAD	Intergovernmental Authority on Development
INCORE	International Conflict Research
MPLA	*Movimento Popular de Libertaçao de Angola*
MPR	*Mouvement Populaire de la Révolution* (Popular Revolutionary Movement)
NCCR	Swiss National Centre for Competence in Research
NDDC	Niger-Delta Development Commission
NGOs	non-governmental organizations
RCD	Congolese Assembly for Democracy
RCD-ML	Congolese Rally for Democracy – Liberation Movement
OMPADEC	Oil Mineral Producing Areas Development Commission
OPC	Oduduwa People's Congress
PKOs	peacekeeping operations

RPP	Reflecting on Peace Practice Project
RWI	Rwandan Women's Initiative UN
SADC	Southern African Development Community
SADF	South African Defence Force
SAP	Structural Adjustment Programme
SAWPO	South West Africa People's Organization
SPDC	Shell Petroleum Development Company
UMP	Urban Management Programme
UNDP	United Nations Development Programme
UNESCO	United Nations Educational, Scientific and Cultural Organization
UNFPA	United Nations Population Fund
UNHCR	United Nations High Commission for Refugees
UNICEF	United Nations Children's Fund
UNIFEM	United Nations Development Fund for Women
UNITA	*Uniao Nacional para a Independencia Total de Angola*
USAID	US Agency for International Development
USAID/OTI	United States Agency for International Development/Office of Transition Initiatives
UNCRC	United Nations Convention on the Rights of the Child
UNHCR	UN High Commissioner for Refugees
UNTAG	United Nations Transitions Assistance Group
WCRWC	Women's Commission for Refugee Women and Children
WFP	World Food Programme

Contributors

Bolanle Akande Adetoun has a BSc in General Agriculture, an MPhil in Agricultural Extension and Rural Sociology, and a PhD in Rural Sociology from Obafemi Awolowo University, Ile-Ife, Nigeria. Additionally, she had post-doctoral training in Demography from Cornell University Ithaca, New York. She lectured at Obafemi Awolowo University, Ile-Ife, then headed the Planning, Research and Statistics Department of the National Centre for Women's Development, Abuja, Nigeria. In 1999, she was the Director for the Annual Gender Institute of the Council for the Development of Social Science Research in Africa (CODESRIA) Dakar, Senegal. From 1997–2004, she coordinated the activities of the Centre for Sustainable Development and Gender Issues (CESDEG), Abuja, Nigeria. Her research focus includes Gender Issues, Population and Reproductive Health, Agriculture, Social and Rural Development. She is currently the Head of Gender Division for the Economic Community of West African States (ECOWAS).

Dominic Agyeman is a Professor of Sociology at the University of Cape Coast, Ghana. He has been involved in the Policy Project funded by USAID, and has worked on the Population Council. He has published in the areas of population control, fertility, and ethnic conflict in divided societies.

Isaac Olawale Albert is a Reader in Peace and Conflict Studies at the Institute of African Studies, University of Ibadan, Nigeria. He initiated and served as the Nigerian coordinator of the academic link between INCORE and the University of Ibadan in Peace and Conflict Studies. The DFID-sponsored link, among many other things, led to the commencement of the academic course of the University of Ibadan in Peace and Conflict Studies, which Dr. Albert coordinates. Dr. Albert is a professional mediator and has participated in conflict management projects in different parts of Nigeria, Africa, Europe, the Middle East, and the US. He is a Board Member of the West African Network for Peacebuilding (Accra, Ghana) and the Board Chairman of the organization in Nigeria. He has published extensively on issues pertaining to peace and conflict in Africa.

Erin K. Baines received a PhD in International Studies from Dalhousie University in 2000. She is currently the Director of the Conflict and Development Programme at the Liu Institute for Global Issues, University of British Columbia in Vancouver, Canada. She is the author of *Vulnerable Bodies: Gender, the UN and the Global Refugee Crisis* (Ashgate Publishing, London 2004) and was awarded the Henry Frank Guggenheim Prize for her essay on the Role of Academic Research in Reducing Violent Conflict. Her current work focuses on strengthening traditional mechanisms for peace in Northern Uganda.

Arsène Mwaka Bwenge has a Masters in Political Science. He is an Assistant and Researcher in the Department of Political Science and the Centre for Political Studies at the University of Kinshasa, Democratic Republic of the Congo.

Jacqui Gallinetti was admitted as an attorney of the High Court of South Africa in 1995. She has a BA LLB LLM from the University of Cape Town. She practices as an attorney and specializes in criminal law, family law, and representing children in Children's Courts. She joined the children's rights project at the community law centre, University of the Western Cape in 2001 as the project co-ordinator and senior researcher. She is editor of the project's quarterly child justice newsletter, *Article 40*, and co-ordinator of the Child Justice Alliance. She has recently co-edited a book entitled *Child Justice in Africa: A Guide to Good Practice*, and has attended numerous workshops and conferences in a number of African countries relating various aspects of children's rights.

Eghosa Osaghae is Professor of Political Science and Vice Chancellor of Igbinedion University, Nigeria. Previously, he was Leader of the Ford Foundation-funded Programme on Ethnic and Federal Studies and Director of the Centre for Peace and Conflict Studies at the University of Ibadan. From 1995–1998, he was Professor and Head of the Department of Political Studies at the University of Transkei, South Africa. He has been a visiting fellow to the Carter Centre of Emory University (1989), University of Liberia (1989/90), University of Cape Town (1994), the Nordic African Institute (1994), Northwestern University (2002), and University of Cambridge (2003). He has been a Rockefeller Fellow, and was most recently a MacArthur Fellow. In 1996, he won the "Best Paper Award" at the Eighth annual conference of the International Association for Conflict Management at Helsignor, Denmark. He has published extensively on ethnicity, federalism, governance, and state politics. Amongst his books are *Between State and Civil Society in Africa* (1994), *The Management of the National Question in Nigeria* (2001), *Structural Adjustment and Ethnicity in Nigeria* (1995), *Ethnicity, Class and State Power in Liberia* (1995), and *Crippled Giant: Nigeria Since Independence* (1998). His articles have appeared in *Journal of Peace Research, Peace Review, Journal of Commonwealth and Comparative Politics, Nations and Nationalism, Nationalism and Ethnic Politics, Publius: Journal of Federalism, Journal of Modern African Studies, International Journal of World Peace*, and *Journal of Third World Studies*.

Elisabeth Porter is INCORE Research Director. Previously, she has taught at the University of Ulster, Flinders University of South Australia, the University of South Australia and Southern Cross University, Australia where she taught, "Peace, War and International Politics". She has published on women, political decision-making and peace-building; security and inclusiveness; citizenship, pluralism, diversity and democratic dialogue; and the political representation of women in Northern Ireland. She is the author of three books (*Feminist Perspectives on Ethics, Building Good Families, Women and Moral Identity*), is co-editor of another book (*Activating Human Rights*). She is writing a book on *Women*

and Peace-building: Ideas and Practices.

Gillian Robinson is Director of INCORE (International Conflict Research www.incore.ulster.ac.uk) at the University of Ulster and Director of ARK (The Northern Ireland Social and Political Archive www.ark.ac.uk). She is the 2003 Eisenhower Fellow from Northern Ireland. She has been involved in the monitoring of social attitudes in Northern Ireland since 1989 and co-directs the Northern Ireland Life and Times survey series. Her research interests include social attitudes, gender roles, policy development in transition, and research methodology, including issues around researching violent societies and comparative methods. She has published extensively on these issues including six books and numerous articles.

Albrecht Schnabel is a Senior Research Fellow at swisspeace, Bern, and a Lecturer in International Organizations and Conflict Management at the Institute of Political Science, University of Bern. In addition to academic and policy-oriented research and training in the areas of peace-building and human security, he is involved in a backstopping mandate on Swiss peace policy for the Swiss Federal Department of Foreign Affairs. He was educated at the University of Munich, the University of Nevada, and Queen's University, Canada, where he received his PhD in Political Studies in 1995. He has held academic positions at the American University in Bulgaria, the Central

European University, Aoyama Gakuin University, Tokyo, and, most recently, the United Nations University. He has published widely on ethnic conflict, conflict prevention and management, peacekeeping, peace-building, refugees, and humanitarian intervention.

Marie Smyth is Head of Research and Communication for Criminal Justice Inspection Northern Ireland, and Chair of the government's Research Ethics Committee 1 for Northern Ireland. She was 2002–2003 Jennings Randolph Senior Fellow in the US Institute of Peace and founder and CEO of the Institute for Conflict Research from 1994–2003. Her research on conflict in West and Southern Africa, the Middle East, and Northern Ireland has led to a range of books and articles on topics including: the humanitarian, social, and political impact of armed conflict; the militarization of young people; victims' politics; truth recovery; demilitarization; paramilitary groups; and research ethics.

J. Zoë Wilson completed her Doctorate in Political Science at Dalhousie University, Canada, in May 2004. Her dissertation, entitled "Wishful Thinking, Wilful Blindness and Artful Amnesia: UN Programs to Promote Good Governance Democracy and Human Rights in Africa", traced global norms and aspirations down to four country cases: Angola, Botswana, Namibia, and Tanzania. Zoë's chapter in this volume was born of fieldwork in Angola in 2001. Zoë is currently a post-doctoral fellow at the Centre for Civil Society at the University of KwaZulu Natal in Durban, South Africa, and a Senior Research Fellow at the Institute for Research and Innovation in Sustainability (IRIS) at York University, Canada. Current research projects seek to map the role of international actors and institutions in South Africa's municipal water delivery architecture. Recent publications include chapters in books and articles in *Journal of Peacebuilding and Development* 2(1) Dec 2004 and *Politikon* 31(1) May 2004.

Introduction

Eghosa Osaghae and Gillian Robinson

Africa has the uncanny reputation of being the world's leading theatre of conflict, war, poverty, disease, and instability. Therefore it is not surprising that scholars of ethnicity and conflict management regard it as a major laboratory for experimentation and theory building. Notwithstanding the exaggerations and oversimplifications that sometimes attend the claims and findings, including the tendency to lump all states in the continent together as suffering from the tribalism disease, Africa generally has not disappointed and, in a manner of speaking, has lived up to its billing. This is certainly true of the turbulent post-Cold War period in which Africa has experienced persistent violent and seemingly intractable conflicts.

The notorious genocide and ethnic cleansing in Rwanda and to some extent Burundi, civil wars in Liberia, Sierra Leone, the Democratic Republic of Congo, Sudan, Côte d'Ivoire and Somalia, minority uprisings in Nigeria, and separatist agitation in Cameroon and Senegal, represent reference points of the turbulence in the African continent. In addition, conflicts of varying magnitudes, mostly local but no less state-threatening have ravaged many other countries including Ghana, Zambia, and Benin which were regarded for a long time as peaceful and less prone to deadly conflicts. Although the conflicts generally have deep historical roots that date back to the colonial and even pre-colonial periods, they became more prevalent and destructive in the post-Cold War period.

As expected, the wind of violent conflicts blowing across Africa has attracted the attention of scholars. Two aspects of the conflicts have

1

been of particular interest to researchers, namely the explanation of the deterioration of the conflict situation and the management of the conflicts. Those who consider the explanation of the increase in prevalence and intensity of conflict to be the main priority of research have identified a range of key precipitants, such as the contradictions of globalization and the attendant intensification of identity-based struggles for control of power and resources, contradictions of simultaneous economic and political reforms, difficulties in transition, flawed democratization, declining state capacities and diminishing resources and the proliferation of small arms. Yet, although we now know a lot about the "causes" and nature of conflicts, they remain intractable and difficult to predict and to deal with. This has implications for the management of conflict, which has been the other area of research interest.

Although some of the notable and fairly successful cases have been highlighted, the South African "miracle", Ethiopia's ethnic federalism, Botswana's democratic stability, sub-regional approaches to conflicts via the Economic Community of West African States (ECOWAS), Inter-governmental Authority on Development (IGAD), Southern African Development Community (SADC), and more recently the African Union (AU), a dismal picture of inability, failure, and hopelessness generally is painted.

Indeed, some analysts have given up and gone ahead to advocate "rethinking" the state in Africa, including the dissolution or disintegration of so-called troublesome and unviable states, as possible alternatives (Clapham, 2001). Others have called for creative and innovative approaches, including the adaptation of traditional models and practices (Zartman, 2000). The problem, however, is that the management of conflict literature does not adequately reflect or acknowledge the efforts made in a number of countries to deal with conflicts. It is probably true that the overall state of war, crisis, and instability overwhelms whatever successes may have been recorded, but the point nevertheless remains that there are management dimensions and interventions that have yet to be fully interrogated. These would hopefully show that conflict management in Africa is not altogether the "hopeless case" that is painted in the mostly pessimistic perspectives that dominate the literature.

One point that emerges from this brief overview is that although extant research on ethnic conflicts in Africa has covered a lot of ground, a lot more work still needs to be done. In fact, the new and evolving forms and patterns of ethnic nationalism and conflicts that have characterized the post-Cold War period, notably the upsurge of minority agitations, aggravated politics of difference and contested citizenship, and the importance of issues of globalization, resource control, environmental justice, and state reconfiguration have thrown up new challenges to conventional wisdoms that demand innovative and alternative prisms and perspectives. Fortuitously, scholars have risen to the challenge as the field has been reworked and new paradigms and approaches to the explanation of conflict and management of conflict have emerged within the larger framework of research on transitions and African development (Himmelstrand et al., 1994; Joseph, 1999; Osaghae, 1995, 2004; Zeleza, 1997).

With specific regard to ethnic conflict, several methodological issues, some new and some not so new but previously taken for granted or ignored by researchers have come under scrutiny as analysts try to capture and explain the changing scenarios of violent societies. These range from such old but basic fundamentals about the actual nature of ethnicity and ethnic conflicts in terms of whether identities are constructed or "natural" and whether conflicts that are termed ethnic are masks for more underlying (class, religious, and economic competition-based) conflicts, to gender dimensions of conflict, and the roles of the state, civil society, the international community, and forces of globalization in the instigation and management of conflicts, peace-building, and state reconfiguration.

The nature of recent conflicts and interventions to manage or resolve them has also made ethical considerations a key methodological issue. Ethical considerations are of course not new in researching conflicts in violent societies. Researchers involved in or doing participatory/action research, participant observation, peace-building/conflict resolution, and humanitarian assistance, normally are required to observe the rules of confidentiality, especially with regard to disclosures, in order to maintain objectivity and accountability. But although these rules are fairly well known and researchers try hard to abide by them, a number of ethical dilemmas remain and have in fact become more pressing with the outburst of violent conflicts requiring "outsider" intervention.

For instance, should the protection of members of vulnerable groups (women, children, the aged, and the physically challenged) be at the expense, as it were, of fighting soldiers who may be and frequently are victims themselves, but are held to be instigators or gladiators in conflict and war situations? Should human rights considerations, which have now formed a part of the global ethical code of good governance, sway the researcher to the side of just struggles of oppressed minorities against state and majoritarian tyranny? Stated in terms like these, ethical considerations ought to be central to conflict research in Africa, but so far they have not received the attention they so clearly deserve. The consequences of the resultant absence of "responsible" research can be well imagined. It may very well be that the inability of research to impact proactively and positively on conflicts in Africa, lead instead to complicating interventions as in Sierra Leone and the Democratic Republic of Congo, which are explicable in these terms.

These are some of the emerging themes that were taken up at the workshop on ethical and methodological issues in researching violent societies held at the University of Ibadan, Nigeria, in February 2002 and from which papers in this volume have been selected. The workshop was part of an ongoing series of work into the issue of "Researching Divided Societies" based at INCORE (International Conflict Research) at the University of Ulster in Northern Ireland, and brought together researchers on African conflicts from inside and outside the continent to address the various issues and challenges of researching violent societies in the post-Cold War period and how they may be tackled. By bringing the workshop to Africa, the organizers hoped to provide an opportunity for researchers on the continent to engage recent and ongoing methodological debates and dialogues. This was a deliberate response to the unfortunate trend in African studies that allows researchers on the continent to be bypassed and ignored in the production of knowledge about their societies (Zeleza, 1997). In addition, it was also an opportunity to begin the mainstreaming of ethical issues and dilemmas in the research agenda of African scholars. As noted above, ethical issues are undeveloped in African conflict studies, having been neglected or taken for granted all along. This state of affairs, it goes without saying, is no longer tenable if we hope to respond adequately to the many challenges posed by the pervasive regime of violent conflicts on the continent.

The book covers many issues and represents case studies from indigenous researchers' experiences together with accounts of the experience of "outsider" researchers. Many of the issues are common to research in any divided society but are magnified in the African situation. In Part 1 Marie Smyth focuses on insider-outsider issues and is followed by Albrecht Schnabel who explores how we ensure conflict research actually impacts on policy and on the prevention of conflict. Part 2 presents the case studies. In Chapters 3–7 indigenous researchers from across Africa raise key questions. Bolanle Adetoun begins by identifying key roles and responsibilities for research and the researcher in a divided society. Drawing on a case study of the Niger Delta region, she argues that research that is properly planned, executed, disseminated, and utilized is vital for divided societies. Dominic Agyeman takes the argument further by calling for a Convention on Conflict Studies to guide researchers involved in conflict studies. Isaac Olawale Albert in his chapter discusses the sensitive issue of studying militia movements and raises serious ethical issues that form a thread running through the book. Arsène Mwaka Bwenge drawing from his experience in the Democratic Republic of Congo stresses the need to use "living techniques" to allow the actors and witnesses involved in the change to speak. The importance of research into and involving children living in divided and violent societies is raised by Jacqui Gallinetti who argues that it is our duty as researchers to ensure the child's voice is heard. Part 2 concludes with two chapters from outsiders who have conducted their research in Africa. Zoë Wilson demonstrates the dangers of exclusion of people from the research process and Erin Baines highlights the importance of inclusive gendered analyses.

Finally, Elisabeth Porter reflects on the directions of research in Africa in the conclusion.

The contributors to this volume and the Researching Divided Societies programme continue to explore these complex and important issues. The topic was also the focus of a seminar and workshop in Bogota, Colombia in 2003 and we hope to convene further meetings elsewhere. We conclude, as we did in our earlier book (Smyth, 2001: 11): "Researchers working in the field bear the responsibility of conducting research in the most effective and ethical way possible, in order that such learning can be maximized, and perhaps some future violence avoided. There can be little work that is more crucial".

REFERENCES

Clapham, Christopher, ed. (2001) *Regional Integration in Southern Africa: Comparative International Perspectives*, Johannesburg: South African Institute of International Affairs in Collaboration with the Nordic Council of Ministry and the British High Commission in Pretoria.

Himmelstrand, Ulf, Kinyanjui, Kabiru, and Mburugu, Edward, eds. (1994) *African Perspectives on Development: Controversies, dilemmas and opening*, Nairobi: EAEP; London: James Currey.

Joseph, Richard (1999) *State, Conflict and Democracy in Africa*, Boulder Colo.: Lynne Rienner.

Osaghae, Eghosa (1995) "The Study of Political Transitions in Africa", *Review of African Political Economy* 22(64): 183–197.

——— (2004) "Political Transitions and Ethnic Conflict in Africa", *Journal of Third World Studies* 21(1): 221–240.

Smyth, Marie (2001) "Introduction", in Marie Smyth and Gillian Robinson, eds., *Researching Violently Divided Societies: Ethical and Methodological Issues*, London: Pluto Press/Tokyo: United Nations University Press, pp. 1–11.

Zartman, William, ed. (2000) *Traditional Cures for Modern Conflicts: African Conflict "Medicine"*, Boulder, Colo.: Lynne Rienner.

Zeleza, Paul Tiyambe (1997) *Manufacturing African Studies and Crisis*, Dakar: CODESRIA Books.

I

Researching violently divided societies: Ethical, methodological, and policy issues

1

Insider–outsider issues in researching violent and divided societies

Marie Smyth

My involvement with research on conflict began as an insider, with my research on Northern Ireland (Smyth, 2004a; Smyth and Fay, 2000; Smyth et al., 1999; Smyth, Hamilton, and Thomson, 2002; Smyth and Morrissey, 2002; Smyth, Morrissey, and Fay, 1999; Smyth and Scott, 2000). The methods I used were participatory action research alongside large survey methods and in-depth interviews (Smyth, 2004b). I relied on insider knowledge in the conduct of the research, of the culture and political sensitivities involved in the topic. Yet, I had to forgo my insider identity in that my political views and loyalties to my own group had to be set aside in the interests of more effectively studying a conflict in which my own community was partisan. I have also worked as a researcher in South Africa, Ghana, Macedonia, Israel, and the Occupied Palestinian Territories. In these contexts, I am clearly an outsider, although I can also be an outsider in my own country.

A chapter for a book on researching conflict, ethnicity, and violent divisions in Africa cannot avoid the issue of insiders and outsiders. Describing any contemporary conflict as "ethnic" conflict is an assertion that can, in itself, divide insiders and outsiders. It implies that at least some of the root cause of the conflict lies with the identity of those living inside it. The attribution of "ethnicity" in certain contexts carries with it a cachet of backwardness, primitiveness, and exoticism. Some African scholars have, with good reason, rejected the use of the term "ethnic conflict" when applied to the problems of contemporary Africa, since its use has tended to sidestep causal factors other than the ethnicity of participants.

In Northern Ireland, where I am an "insider", it is not widespread practice to describe the conflict of the last three decades as "ethnic" since such a description relies on the concept of "warring tribes" which would be seen as an over-simplification, and a denial, for example, of the roles of the British and Irish governments. Yet some insiders would accept that there may well be an ethnic dimension to a conflict that primarily is about national identity. Others perceive the "ethnic" description as an obfuscation of the true nature of the conflict.

In the introduction to this volume, Osaghae and Robinson point out that old questions remain unaddressed, to a large extent, in the African context; questions such as social constructionist versus "natural" views of the nature of ethnicity and identity. At both a political and academic level, debates continue between those who assert that "ethnic conflict" masks the underlying nature of the conflict, which is ultimately based on class, religion and economic competition. In analytical terms, other issues have received scant attention, such as the gendered dimensions of conflict, and the roles of the state, civil society and the international community, the role played by global factors in the causation of conflicts, and critical evaluations of the role of internationals – "outsiders" – in the management of conflict, post-conflict reconstruction, peace-building, and state-building.

In the context of Africa, the contemporary understanding of the role of ethnicity in African political life is advanced considerably by the analysis of Udogu (2001) and his contributors. Whereas earlier critiques of the use of the term ethnicity in the context of Africa tended to see ethnicity as the invention of outsiders, without substance, Udogu's book reassesses this view, and revisits the issue of ethnicity in case studies of Kenya, Nigeria, and Sierra Leone. In the same volume, Soyinka-Airewele (2001: 179) comments that: "for the African intellectual it would appear that the starting point in the study and negotiation of multi-ethnic politics must be the abandonment of rigid positions and counterproductive assumptions regarding ethnicity".

Soyinka-Airewele (2001) argues that the term "tribe" still tends to be used as part of a negative stereotype. To caricature the worst aspects of the "ethnic" thesis, it is that "native" people are "primitive", racially or genetically predisposed to fight, and incapable of or unwilling to resolve conflicts themselves. Therefore the task of resolving such conflicts falls to (higher status) outsiders who often regard themselves as "experts" or specialists. Such a scenario contains many risks: of victim-blaming; of producing analysis and intervention that is ahistorical and acontextual; of overlooking local knowledge and savoir-faire; of underestimating "outsider" or expert ignorance or limitations in experience; of making interventions that are inappropriate or a poor cultural or political fit with the specific context; and of seeing violence and conflict as the sole prerogative of developing or less wealthy nations. However, to entirely reject the notion of ethnicity, to refute its relevance entirely is to abandon a potential tool for deepening understanding of some of the dynamics – if not always the root causes – of violent conflict. Violence is ubiquitous, and the study of conflicts in Africa must be placed in the context of that ubiquity. As Nordstrom and Robben (1995: 2) point out:

violence is not somewhere else – in a third world country, on a distant battlefield, or in a secret interrogation center – but an inescapable fact of life for every country, nation, and person, whether or not they are personally touched by direct violence.

Violence, racial attacks, hate-crime and religious conflicts are features of everyday life in developed nations. The streets of New York and London are sites of violence, and life in the developed suburbia is lived in the shadow of the threat of violence, yet Africans do not turn up in the developed world offering themselves as experts in solving problems of violence in the developed world. Interest and intervention in conflict in Africa by outsiders, therefore, is founded on and shaped by the world order, and by power relations between the nations-of-origin of the outsider and the nation they work in.

Merton's (1972) original article on "Insiders and Outsiders" did not define "insiders" solely in terms of nationality or country/continent of origin. Merton argued that within single societies, an insider–outsider dimension could be observed. He wrote, "I adopt a structural conception of Insiders and Outsiders. In this conception, Insiders are the members of specified groups and collectivities or occupants of certain social statuses; Outsiders are non-members" (Merton, 1972: 21). Merton cites Polanyi (1967) who pointed out that the growth of knowledge depends on complex sets of social relations based on reciprocity of trust. Societies and academic communities, however, increasingly are divided by what has come to be called identity politics. Merton, writing in the early 1970s, pointed to the polarization of society on the basis of "insiders" and "outsiders" and the consequent proliferation of movements based on class, race, sex, religion, and sexual orientation. These movements expressed, according to Merton, "public affirmation of pride in certain statuses and of the solidarity with groups that for a long time have been socially degraded, stigmatized, or harassed in other ways by the social system" (1972: 11).

The result has been the (sometimes) rigid consolidation of insider and outsider positions. In Northern Ireland, even though I was working in my own country, I was an "outsider" when I researched the experience of disabled police officers, or the lives of those who lived in segregated enclaves. Not only was I an outsider in terms of not being part of the groups that I studied, I was also separated from them by social class, education, and the position of power that being a researcher entails. Some of the groups I researched have a strong sense of internal solidarity and identity, and clear boundaries between insiders and outsiders. Violent conflict tends to consolidate and reinforce such boundaries, as the wider society polarizes in response to violent attack and counter-attack. Merton's (1972) description of the development of what he refers to as "insider doctrine", which was derived from his observations of racial politics in the United States in the late 1960s and early 1970s, is reminiscent of insider–outsider dynamics in (other) violently divided societies.

Many of Osaghae's and Robinson's points in the introduction to this volume resonate with my own "insider" experience as a native of Northern Ireland, and a researcher of the conflict within my own society, as well as an "outsider" researcher in Africa and the Middle East. I well remember the first time I was able to visit South Africa after the fall of apartheid. Having lived most of my life in a society – Northern Ireland – that is deeply divided, where segregation is a feature of education, housing, and social life, South Africa felt somehow familiar, like home, to me. Others have reported similar experiences. Perhaps it is that we recognize the subtle and not-so-subtle ways in which the divisions are contained and the society is organized. In South Africa, I seemed to know intuitively many of the unspoken rules, because they were so similar to those at home. I was an outsider, but less of an outsider than I am in Sweden or Norway, and less of an outsider than the Swedish or Norwegian person in South Africa. My socialization in a divided society, my years of experience of living with an armed conflict have rendered conflict and societal division familiar to me, a reminder of home.

The value of such experience is undeniable. Some of my most useful thinking about my own society has been stimulated by recognizing, on visits to other divided societies, these commonalities that we in Northern Ireland share with the country I happen to be visiting. Conversely, in deciphering patterns and anticipating issues in other divided societies, the "algebra" of conflict and division that I learned in my own country often assists with understanding other contexts. So perhaps I am an "insider" in a group of those who have experience of living for protracted periods in divided societies. And perhaps "insider" and "outsider" experience is multiple and layered, rather than singular and one-dimensional. Perhaps there is an obverse side to this. My experience of conflict may also blind me to aspects of other societies that I take for granted because of my own immersion in the experience of conflict in my own country. This, in turn raises questions about the baseline from which comparative work on conflict is conducted. Do we operate from some notional benchmarked hypothetical "normal" society or do we merely compare what is normal to us?

It is perhaps inevitable that such groups composed of "insiders" will produce their own insider perspective that departs from the "outsider" views, particularly where the perspective of the group has been regarded as less legitimate. Such insider perspectives often are formed in the context of the marginalization and stigmatization of the group, and can be seen in some ways as a reaction against such marginalization. Merton, however, describes how certain groups, some in the mainstream of society, have historically claimed monopolistic access to particular kinds of knowledge, or, in less extreme cases, some groups claim privileged access to certain knowledge. Merton (1972: 11) cites Marx's description of post-capitalist society ridding itself of false consciousness and the ideology of Nazism:

contrasting the access to authentic scientific knowledge by men of unimpeachable Aryan ancestry with the corrupt versions of knowledge accessible to non-Ayrans ... and ... the new racial category of "white Jews" to refer to those Aryans who had defiled their race by actual or symbolic contact with non-Aryans.

He goes on to describe the de facto insiderism of American academia, which is composed of "patterned expectations about the appropriate selection of specialities and of problems for investigation" (1972: 11).

A more contemporary analysis might suggest, however, that some of the patterning occurs along racial, gender, or class lines, and is more systematic. Yet Merton contrasts this de facto insiderism with an explicitly doctrinal form of insiderism, such as the argument by some black scholars in the United States of America in the 1960s and '70s that only black historians can understand black history, which he summarizes (1972: 15) as:

you have to be one to understand one ... the doctrine holds that one has monopolistic or privileged access to knowledge, or is wholly excluded from it, by virtue of one's group membership or social position.

He points to problems with this doctrinal form of insiderism by extending the argument – only young people can understand young people, only women can understand women, only Jews can understand Jews, and so on. Such extreme insiderism "represents a new credentialism ... of ascribed status,... it contrasts with the credentialism of achieved status of meritocratic systems ... Extreme Insiderism moves towards a doctrine of group methodological solipsism" (ibid.: 14).

For Merton, then, "insider" knowledge is linked inextricably with the solidarity of the insider with his or her group. Added to this is the additional knowledge and insight that the insider possesses, which lead to what he calls the Insider Principle. Merton (ibid.) dismisses the trivial version of the argument ("that the Outsiders may be incompetent, given to quick and superficial forays into the group or culture under study and even unschooled in its language") by pointing out that incompetence, foolishness and poor training is to be found in all groups, and is not exclusively associated with Outsiders. The Insider Principle, he proposes, is (1972: 15):

the belief that no Outsider, no matter how careful and talented, is excluded in principle from gaining access to the social and cultural truth ... the Outsider has a structurally imposed incapacity to comprehend alien groups, statuses, cultures, and societies ... and cannot have the direct, intuitive sensitivity that alone makes empathic understanding possible. Only through continued socialization in the life of a group can one become fully aware of its symbolisms and socially shared realities; only so can one understand the fine-grained meanings of behavior, feelings, and values; only so can one decipher the unwritten grammar of conduct and nuances of cultural idiom.

Merton (1972: 15) points to a "less stringent" version of this position, which holds that insider and outsider scholars have different concerns and foci of interest, because Insiders:

sharing the deepest concerns of the group or at the least being thoroughly aware of them, will so direct their inquiries as to have them be relevant to those concerns ... Unlike the stringent version of the doctrine, which maintains that Insiders and Outsiders must arrive at different (and presumably incompatible) findings and interpretations even when they do examine the same problems, this weaker version argues only that they will not deal with the same questions and so will simply talk past one another.

Merton links this view with ethnocentrism, "the view of things in which one's own group is the center of everything, and all others are scaled and rated with reference to it" (Sumner, 1907: 13).

However, Merton's study analyses the positions of insiders and outsiders simply as intellectual standpoints. If we take into account the impact of violence and war on ways of thinking and ways of knowing, and indeed on identity itself, then the Insider Principle, described above, becomes more understandable. Violence acts as a centrifugal social force, not only polarizing politics, but also creating an intellectual climate in which polarized "black and white" thinking is tolerated, as the intellectual life of a society reflects the political and ideological climate of that society. Consider, for example, the contemporary intellectual divisions in the Middle East, where Israeli "new historians" are ostracized by their Zionist colleagues, where boycotts and threats punctuate academic debate and scholarship on the history and contemporary politics of the region.

In violently divided societies, it is not merely the population that are polarized and segregated, but intellectuals, academics, and researchers reflect the divisions in the society, and bring to the job of the production of ideas their various loyalties. Ideas, too, are separating into "right" and "wrong", making for a marked dualistic thinking which is associated with the earlier stages of intellectual development. All thinkers, when exposed to life-threatening violence, will tend to revert to this form of thinking. It is not the exclusive terrain of insiders. It is a rare researcher, whether insider or outsider, that will, when faced with a threat to his or her life, entirely retain the ability to examine the situation in which the threat occurred with any kind of scientific rigour. The tendency for what Merton referred to as Insider Doctrine to develop can be interpreted in the light of this, and in the context of strong ingroup–outgroup boundaries that are associated with violent conflict. The impact of violence and threat on ways of thinking has implications for the quality of data collection, but particularly for analysis.

It seems, then, that there are two dimensions to the debate about the role and relative capacities of insiders versus outsiders as researchers in violently divided societies. The first is a debate about context, history, colonialism, and power relations sketched out above. The second is a debate about scientific method and concerns the relative merits and effectiveness of insiders versus outsiders as researchers, mediators or analysts.

Scientific method: insider–outsider comparisons

Table 1.1 attempts to summarize and tabulate some of the other comparative advantages and disadvantages faced by indigenous "insider" and external "outsider" researchers, in five key areas:
• Identity management and risk
• Objectivity/subjectivity
• Depth of knowledge
• Cultural competence
• Impact of witnessing

Identity management and risk

Researchers operating in conflict zones must consider issues of their safety and that of their informants. Here, the insider researcher can be

Table 1.1 Insider and outsider effectiveness in researching violently divided societies

Factor	Insider		Outsider	
	Advantage	Disadvantage	Advantage	Disadvantage
Identity management and risk	May know the terrain intimately	Perceived as partial/part of conflict so risk/danger may be greater	Perceived objectivity can improve safety	Lack of detailed knowledge can lead to ignorance of risk
Objectivity/subjectivity	Can be easily located within the society, and his/her analysis read accordingly	May be totally identified with one side and unable to make paradigm shift to studying conflict as a whole	Comparative analysis may be facilitated by researcher's position and knowledge of other societies	Chimera of "objectivity" – outsider researchers are often caught in dynamic of conflict and "take sides"
Depth of knowledge	Greater potential for in-depth knowledge of terrain	Blind spots (both geographically and disciplinarily) may be considerable due to proximity to subject	Potentially able to adopt fresh perspective on the society	a. secondary sources which may be from one predominant perspective due to censorship, etc. b. acquired knowledge/ "book learning" versus experiential learning
Cultural competence	Competence level is likely to be high	Cultural aspects of society that pertain to conflict may be taken for granted and "invisible" to the insider due to over-familiarity	Culture may be highly visible due to lack of over-familiarity	May be liable to misinterpret or be unable to interpret data due to lack of cultural competence

at a distinct advantage, in that they may know the terrain intimately, and have a network of contacts through which they can collect information and monitor issues such as safety. However, this is not equally true of all insiders, and some outsiders are skilled at quickly establishing networks, and finding reliable advisors on issues such as safety. Insiders, too, can accept unquestioningly local superstitions and assumptions about danger and risk, which may not be real. Furthermore, insiders may be perceived as partial, as part of conflict, identified with one or the other side, consequently the risk may be greater. However, insiders are more likely than outsiders to have at their disposal more local resources to mitigate such risk.

Outsider identity can be a mixed blessing. In impoverished areas, researchers who by their skin color or other external markers are identified clearly with the developed world may have to constantly manage the issue of economic inequality, and the perceptions of their personal wealth and access to resources or power. In embattled communities, outsiders can be regarded with a great deal of suspicion, and subjected to intense questioning about their intentions, making it a challenge to establish sufficient trust to carry out the research.

The perception of the outsider researcher as objective or neutral can be a distinct advantage in terms of safety and access to data. However, the researcher may find himself or herself the target of attempted indoctrination into one or the other perspective as a result. Whilst this can be fruitful in terms of data collection, it can be tiresome when it proves to be difficult to deflect more relentless attempts at proselytizing. The major disadvantage faced by outside researchers in relation to safety and risk management is that their relative lack of knowledge of the context and relative inability to interpret cues may leave them ignorant of those actual risks they are taking.

Objectivity and subjectivity

A comparison of the relative merits of insider versus outsider research on violently divided contexts tends to assume certain advantages in each position: greater objectivity on the part of the outsider, and greater in-depth knowledge and understanding of the dynamics on the part of insiders. However, recent work on research in violently divided societies has reaffirmed the myth of objectivity (Smyth and Robinson, 2001). All researchers in violent contexts, whether insider or outsider, bring to their work their own previous identifications and experiences. These inevitably affect the extent to which a researcher identifies with one or the other competing interest in the field of study. However, the influence that these factors exert is not straightforward. Over- or under-compensation for one's identity; the emotional impact of violence and the suffering it causes; over- or under-identification with one cohort; and the failure to adopt a systemic analytic framework can render researchers intellectually and analytically disabled, burnt out and emotionally overwhelmed. These unfortunate fates can befall insider and outsider alike. Violently divided societies often are characterized by geographical and ideological segregation between conflict zones and safer territory, with researchers venturing into the conflict zones in order to do fieldwork, but who usually are living and working in safer territory. The conflict zone is often, therefore, foreign territory to insider and outsider alike. It is perhaps only in the depth of understanding and in the ability to interpret nuance that the abiding difference between insider and outsider researchers lies. Notwithstanding, if outsiders are read locally, they may be perceived – sometimes to the surprise of the author – to be partial to one or the other faction in the conflict, whereas some insiders can achieve the elusive prize of being regarded as objective and even-handed.

There has been a tendency to under-value indigenous or insider research on conflict because of assumptions of bias on the part of indigenous researchers. Some of this tendency is due to institutionalized racism or colonial attitudes. However, assumptions about the superior validity of outsider perspectives are deeply ingrained. This assumption of the superiority of the "outsider" perspective is often couched in arguments about the scientific value in terms of the "objectivity" of the work. Yet, as referred to earlier, the impossibility of objectivity in the field of conflict research is well known. However, the work of the insider as compared to that of the outsider may be addressed to different audiences. The work of the insider may be more valuable in terms of its local intelligibility, and its ability to impact directly on the dynamics of conflict, although elsewhere, we have questioned whether, in fact, research makes any difference to conflict (Darby and Smyth, 2001). The ability of indigenous research to speak to the home audiences about conflict and the ability to affect positive shifts as a result, often is overlooked, taken for granted or under-valued.

The other side of the objectivity coin is the ability of outsiders to remain objective in their research on conflict in a country other than their own. The experience of watching outsider researchers operate in my own country leads me to conclude that outside researchers, more often than not, very quickly identify with one side or the other of the conflict, and consequently their analysis is predictable. Few can resist the pull of the centrifugal force of violence described earlier: researchers do not remain detached or immune from sympathies or loyalty to one side or another. In conducting research in violent societies, it is possible that their living quarters are located in or close to a bombed site, their car is stopped by armed men, their vehicle is hi-jacked or burnt and they respond as most human beings in such circumstances react. Some are more disciplined and rigorous in processing their experiences and using them as research data, attempting to avoid adopting one or the other side. Others barely trouble themselves with such considerations. Outsider researchers, therefore, may at face value seem more likely to be "objective" than insiders, in that the expectation is that they will be able to see the conflict as a whole, and this may be the case. In practical terms, however, this expectation is not always met. However, in spite of this, outside researchers are more likely in some instances to be regarded as credible, "objective" and "scientific" in their work. Indeed, most analysis of conflict does not make explicit the identity of the researcher, resting on the assumption that such questions are irrelevant. Were insider identities to be declared, there is a tendency to question the scientific value of the analysis and question the perspectives, based on the suspicion that insiders may not be able to see the whole picture.

Depth of knowledge

Another area of difference between insider and outsider researchers is the depth of their knowledge of the context. Insiders can bring a wealth of information and insights to the study of their own society. However, it would be dangerous to assume that outsiders cannot surpass certain insiders in terms of their knowledge and understanding of a particular context. Whilst insiders have been socialized into the context, outsiders must work hard at acquisition of contextual and historical knowledge, but that does not mean that outsiders are always the least knowledgeable in this regard. Insiders can be parochial, blind to certain aspects of their society as a result of their proximity and they may lack interest or curiosity about their environment and context. On the other hand, outsiders can be passionately interested, avid readers, ardent scholars, frequent visitors or long-term residents. A possible disadvantage however, is that such scholarship pursued at a distance from the site of study may be over-reliant on secondary sources which may be skewed, due to for example, censorship or propagandizing. Furthermore, knowledge acquired through reading rather than through experience can lack freshness and may not be fully integrated, a problem faced by the studious outsider researcher. The insider, however, may take much of his or her knowledge for granted. Outsiders have the potential advantage of being able to adopt fresh perspective on a situation, and may also bring useful comparative material, which can greatly assist in analysis and indeed in conflict resolution.

Cultural competence

Where there are distinct cultural or linguistic features to a society being studied, the insider is likely to be more competent than the outsider, although again this cannot be taken for granted. In multi-lingual societies, insiders too, may be at a linguistic disadvantage, and some outsiders make strenuous efforts to learn or improve their linguistic abilities. The major disadvantage faced by the insider is that certain cultural aspects – perhaps relevant to the conflict being studied – may be "invisible" to indigenous researchers, who may be so enculturated that he or she takes these aspects for granted. To the outsider, on the other hand, the insider culture is likely to be highly visible, due to its lack of familiarity, although the outsider may be unable to access data through a lack of skill in negotiating the specific cultural context. Outsiders, too may be liable to misinterpret or unable to interpret data due to lack of knowledge or cultural competence.

Impact of witnessing

One of the challenges in conflict research is the impact of such research on the researcher themselves. In my research in my society, which involved auditing the human impact of political violence on victims and witnesses, my team and I experienced some psychological symptoms (Smyth, 2004b). Whilst the perception may be that insiders have the advantage of habitual acceptance to levels of violence, in reality, the likelihood is that insider researchers usually live and work in relatively safe and secure environments at some distance from the conflict. Therefore, they can be as much at risk from psychological traumatization and other emotional impacts as outsiders. Inexperienced outsider researchers from peaceful societies may be particularly at risk, although there are also personality factor differences involved in levels of vulnerability. There may be differences between insiders and outsiders in terms of their access to those support networks which may offer some protection. However, insiders living and researching an active conflict may have no such access, since psychological impact is often ignored until the post-conflict period, and support services are rarely in place until the conflict is well on its way to resolution. Insiders also face the potential disadvantage of increased emotional proximity to subject, which may increase their risk of traumatization. However, it is not safe to assume that outsiders (such as me, working in the Middle East) do not have previous traumatic experiences in relation to conflict that make them similarly vulnerable, or indeed "hardened" or burnt out. These points notwithstanding, outsiders may well enjoy the advantage of some emotional distance from the subject and their comparative experience may have some prophylactic effect.

Conclusions

The work of external or outsider researchers often is not accessible to insiders, particularly in the developing world. Outsiders' research, however, can sometimes looks facile to insiders' eyes and their work may not be useful locally because it fails to contribute anything new or lacks depth. Some outsider researchers have been guilty of writing for outside international audiences, without attempting to make their work accessible to the local people about whom they write. Such material is unlikely to have a positive impact of any kind on the ground. There are notable exceptions to this, of course, and some outsiders make useful and thoughtful contributions to local thinking about some conflicts.

Other strategies can be used by both insiders and outsiders to improve the coverage of their data and the robustness of their analysis. Use of comprehensive quantitative data, such as censuses of deaths or injuries, collected according to transparent and pre-agreed frameworks and analyzed by region, perpetrator, victim identity and so on, can provide useful overviews of a conflict. This is work that can be undertaken by either insiders or outsiders. Alongside this, qualitative data can provide depth of coverage, and analysis can address multiple "realities" explaining conflict in all its complexity and contradictions. This is an argument for the development of methodological approaches to conflict research that assist the researcher to get closer to the subject of study, and a plea for methodological forums in which outsiders and insiders can learn from one another.

In the end, much of the difficulty and advantage faced by researchers whether outsiders or insiders, depends on their personality, level and depth of previous experience, age, cultural background, research competence and level of sensitivity to local contexts. There are, however, some distinct disadvantages to both outsider and insider status. However, some of the disadvantages can be overcome by working in partnership with the "other", with research partnerships of insiders and outsiders working collaboratively as is the case in this book. This is an approach advocated by Hermann (2001) and Merton (1977). Merton advises that "it is necessary that you unite the 'insiders' with the 'outsiders'. You will all have nothing to lose except your own pretensions. In exchange you will have a world of understanding to gain" (1977: 201).

In the context of Africa, such insider–outsider partnerships must be based on mutual respect for each others' scholarship, knowledge and expertise. It must also be based on an open acknowledgement of the very different resources brought to the research task by insiders and outsiders that include differentials of economic support for conflict research and the equally huge differentials in the distribution of different forms of knowledge. Such respectful partnerships are potentially mutually beneficial to both insiders and outsiders, and contribute to greater understanding of conflict and prospects for conflict resolution.

REFERENCES

Darby, John and Smyth, Marie (2001) "Does research make any difference? The case of Northern Ireland", in Marie Smyth and Gillian Robinson, eds., *Researching Violently Divided Societies: Ethical and Methodological Issues*, London: Pluto Press/Tokyo: United Nations University Press, pp. 34–54.

Hermann, Tamar (2001) "The Impermeable Identity Wall: The study of violent conflicts by 'Insiders' and 'Outsiders'", in Marie Smyth and Gillian Robinson, eds., *Researching Violently Divided Societies: Ethical and Methodological Issues*, London: Pluto Press/Tokyo: United Nations University Press, pp. 77–91.

Merton, Robert K. (1972) "Insiders and outsiders: a chapter in the sociology of knowledge", *American Journal of Sociology* 77(July): 9–47.

Nordstrom, Carolyn and Robben, Antonius C.G.M. (1995) *Fieldwork Under Fire: Contemporary Studies of Violence and Survival*, Berkeley: University of California Press.

Polanyi, Michael (1967) *The Tacit Dimension*, London: Routledge Kegan Paul.

Smyth, Marie (2004a) *The Impact of Political Conflict on Children in Northern Ireland: A Report on the Community Conflict Impact on Children Study*, Belfast: Institute for Conflict Research.

Smyth, Marie (2004b) "Using participative action research with war affected populations: lessons from research in Northern Ireland and South Africa", in Marie Smyth and Emma Williamson, eds., *Researchers and Their "Subjects": Ethics, Power Knowledge and Consent*, Bristol: Policy Press, pp. 137–156.

Smyth, Marie and Fay, Marie-Therese (2000) *Personal Accounts of Northern Ireland's Troubles: Public Chaos, Private Loss*, London: Pluto Press.

Smyth, Marie and Morrissey, Michael (2002) *Northern Ireland After the Good Friday Agreement: Victims, Grievance and Blame*, London: Pluto Press.

Smyth, Marie and Robinson, Gillian, eds. (2001) *Researching Violently Divided Societies: Ethical and Methodological Issues*, London: Pluto Press; and Tokyo: United Nations University Press.

Smyth, Marie and Scott, M. (2000) *The YouthQuest 2000 Survey: Young People's Experiences and View of Life in Northern Ireland*, Derry/Londonderry, INCORE/United Nations University and University of Ulster.

Smyth, Marie, Hamilton, Jennifer, and Thomson, Kirsten (2002) *Creggan Community Restorative Justice: An Evaluation and Suggested Way Forward*, Belfast: Institute for Conflict Research.

Smyth, Marie, Morrissey, Michael, and Fay, Marie-Therese (1999) *Northern Ireland's Troubles: The Human Costs*, London: Pluto Press.

Smyth, Marie, Fay, Marie-Therese, Morrissey, Michael, and Wong, Tracey (1999) *Report on the Northern Ireland Survey: The Experience and Impact of the Troubles*, Derry/Londonderry, INCORE/United Nations University and University of Ulster.

Soynika-Airewele, Peyi (2001) "Western discourse and the socio-political pathology of ethnicity in contemporary Africa", in Emmanuel Ike Udogu, ed., *The Issue of Political Ethnicity in Africa*, Aldershot: Ashgate, pp. 160–177.

Sumner, William Graham (1907) *Folkways*, Boston: Ginn.

Udogu, Emmanuel Ike, ed. (2001) *The Issue of Political Ethnicity in Africa*, Aldershot: Ashgate.

2

Preventing and managing violent conflict: The role of the researcher

Albrecht Schnabel

Introduction

Researchers working in universities and research institutions worldwide play an important role in the promotion of both conflict and peace in our contemporary global community: they not only educate and advise many of those who have the power and resources to bring tremendous violence and destruction to their communities, but they also educate and advise those who create and defend structures and processes that transform potential and actual violence into constructive and peaceful cooperation – at local, national, and international levels.

The international community faces great difficulties in managing violent conflict. Local, national, and international actors are struggling to resolve internal wars or such intangible threats as international terrorism. The only feasible and practical alternative to the management of violence is its early prevention. Preventing violent conflict requires *early recognition* of root causes; *early warning* about impending instability and disintegration; and suitable *early responses* to alleviate the potential for the outbreak of violent conflict. Universities and research institutions can play a crucial part in assisting the international community in its efforts to stem the tide of violence, inequality, and injustice which today affect the vast majority of the world's population.

In this chapter, I will focus on the challenges as well as the opportunities that local, national, and international actors face in designing and implementing early recognition, warning, and response. I will then discuss how research and education can contribute to the alleviation of violence. Researchers and educators in societies at risk can play a particu-ularly important role in assisting societies and decision-makers in finding feasible responses before, during, and after violent conflict, at local, national, regional, and global levels. I argue that researchers have the moral duty to attempt to improve the situation on the ground, and to communicate their results effectively to relevant authorities at local, national, and regional/international policy levels. Efforts have to be pooled effectively to maximize limited resources and opportunities for regional and local coordination of knowledge and expertise. The final section of this chapter discusses how regional centres of excellence can play crucial roles in maximizing and enhancing the local expertise that is required for increasing awareness and capacity to address the root causes of violence and injustice in societies at risk. This chapter is relevant to all researchers in violently divided societies.

The challenge: societies at risk and the prevention of violent conflict

The events of 11 September 2001 and the subsequent US-led political, economic, and military campaign against terrorism have taught us an important lesson that in the absence of justice, development, and responsible good governance, "uncivil" society will thrive in the shadow of sometimes very legitimate grievances that are not expressed through constructive and non-violent channels of political and social interaction. While good governance and development will not eradicate the desire of a few to bring great havoc upon others and their own people, it will certainly remove the explicit and implicit popular support that terrorist groups enjoy and on which they depend as they search for funding, places to hide and train, and for combatants that are willing to sacrifice their lives for their beliefs and convictions.

What is it that makes fragile or war-torn societies so receptive to the use and support of violence as a means to bring about political and social change? Divided and conflict-torn societies experience the severe breakdown of economic, political, and social relations between groups and individual citizens. Weak societies need strong and legitimate institutions to help (re)build trust, confidence and to invest in a more stable future. Yet, weak and divided societies cannot easily produce strong and legitimate governments (Schnabel, 2003). International organizations have been assisting societies that have emerged from violent conflict in building their own institutions (such as by organizing and monitoring democratic elections in Bosnia, Kosovo, East Timor, El Salvador, Afghanistan, or

Iraq), or even by replacing those institutions with a trusteeship until the political environment is safe enough – and the domestic civic culture is mature enough – to maintain peaceful political processes.

Yet, preventing violence is of course preferable to stopping it once it has erupted, or to rebuilding societies once they have been devastated by war. Violent conflicts result from long-term instability and insecurity that are usually predictable, highly visible, and curable. Warning signals for societies at risk of violent internal conflict are well-known and documented (Baker and Ausink, 1996; Ball, 1996; Carnegie Commission on Preventing Deadly Conflict, 1997: 44; Esty et al., 1995). If we take these warning signals seriously, then prevention of long-term structural causes of violent conflict would require, among others, the following actions:
- Reduction of demographic pressures;
- Support of transitions to democracy;
- Assurance that the ethnic composition of ruling authorities reflects divisions within the population at large;
- Sufficient and broad provision of public services;
- Stabilization of the national economy and creation of even economic development along all ethnic intergroup and social lines;
- Resolution of long-standing intergroup grievances and facilitation of reconciliation; and
- Prevention of human flight and creation of an attractive environment for local talent and expertise.

In peaceful societies, these and other basic security needs are met by the state, a responsible government, and nonstate actors.[1] In societies at risk (marked by political and economic instability and considerable inter-group or class frictions), external support, assistance, and, if necessary, intervention are required to help overcome the root causes of their problems.[2] However, there are many obstacles to effective preventive action, such as:
- The attention to pending or emerging problems is usually side-tracked by more highly visible emergencies;
- State sovereignty limits external involvement for the prevention or resolution of internal problems, particularly at pre-conflict stages;
- No commonly accepted legal definition of intervention in pre-conflict situations (when, how, why, and who) has so far emerged;
- Financial resources and political will are not easily available when it concerns the prevention of potential crises;
- There is limited access to intelligence and fact-finding, and therefore inadequate high-quality and dependable early warning and analysis of risk assessment;
- There is a lack of coherence and coordination between and within relevant nonstate, state, and interstate actors; and

- Cooperation among all relevant stakeholders (particularly local civil society) is often limited.

These problems can only be overcome with concerted, coordinated, sustainable peace support strategies and efforts by the international community and local actors. Academic institutions have constructive and supporting roles to play in these efforts. Yet, in regions and countries marred by violence, research into the roots of violence and possible mitigation strategies is weak, if not totally absent. As Osaghae notes, "[i]t must count as one of the shortfalls of conflict management in Africa that, even in those countries which have experienced the most devastating conflicts, there are no specialized research institutions dealing with conflicts, including ethnic conflicts" (2001: 25). He further argues (2001: 25) that:

[i]t may be an exaggeration to hold the absence of research bodies or networks responsible for the prevalence of conflict ... [yet] the basic state of conflict management which leaves violent repression and confrontation as the current centrepiece of conflict management practice can be attributed to that absence.

While Osaghae observes that serious research into violent conflict and its management is on the rise, especially as a result of donor attention to violent conflict in Africa throughout the 1980s and 1990s, many sporadic and ad hoc efforts have not yet come together to learn in a concerted way from "one of the most potentially fruitful laboratories for the production of knowledge on conflict situations in general, and ethnic conflicts in particular" (2001: 13). Yet, rigid, well-funded, ethically conducted, and effectively disseminated research (all these points will be discussed further down) can be a significant contribution to the prevention of violence and sustainable efforts to support and consolidate peace in divided societies, a subject to which we will now turn.

The response: sustainable peace support strategies

What is meant by the term "sustainable peace support strategies"? "Sustainable peace" is a synonym for positive peace. While *negative peace* indicates the absence of direct violence, *positive peace* means much more than that: it stands for the creation of conditions for justice, equality, a participatory political system – and other instruments of good governance and meaningful citizenship. Peace support strategies are aimed at preventing, containing, and ending violence – and restoring sustainable peace in its aftermath.[3]

The *actors* involved in this enterprise include: individuals; civil society organizations (local and international); states; subregional organizations; regional organizations; the United Nations and its programmes, agencies, and institutions; and the World Bank, IMF, and regional financial institutions.[4] The *methods* and *tools* for sustainable peace support strategies include political approaches (official "track one" and unofficial "track two/three" diplomacy);[5] economic approaches (aid, assistance, access to markets, and sanctions); and military approaches (armed intervention, peace enforcement, peacekeeping, post-conflict security provision, and security sector transformation). The *timing* of involvement is either during pre-escalation, after the eruption of violence, or after a settlement has been reached. The *duration* of peace support strategies is either continuous and proactive, or ad hoc and reactive.

What is the *feasibility* of "sustainable" peace support strategies? Unfortunately, peace support offered so far has been mostly reactive; ad hoc (if external interest is triggered, usually in response to a direct threat); of limited duration; highly selective; poorly coordinated across the pre-/during-/post-conflict continuum; erratic; politicized and, thus, not sustainable.[6] Peace support strategies can only be sustainable when negative peace is *assured* and positive peace is *generated*. This is a tremendous task: negative peace can be brought about by *coercion*; it can be forced upon a community. Positive peace, however, has to be carefully *crafted*. It is both fortunate and unfortunate that preventive strategies at the post-conflict stage are more feasible. At this stage, the threats are known, conflict causes are better understood, external attention is already assured, and conflict-governments have been struck down or replaced by generally more modest political forces. Post-conflict societies are by no means easy terrain for nation-building and development efforts. Yet the opportunities for targeted mitigation strategies of conflict causes are far greater than during the pre-war phase. On the other hand, the destruction in both material and human terms is also much greater. This suggests a rather perverse conclusion – effective conflict management may require the actual experience of violence, assisting the peacemaker with the lessons learned about why, when, and how a stable or semi-stable situation escalated into destructive violence (Schnabel, 2002: 24–25). While this may make sense from empirical and operational points of view, it makes little sense from normative and moral perspectives. Nevertheless, post-conflict prevention may help in preventing the resurgence of further conflict. There is merit in achieving at least that goal. Past conflicts can be studied, understood, and avoided through relevant mitigation mechanisms.

The contribution of research to early warning and early response to conflict escalation and consolidation

Research and thorough knowledge are not panaceas to preventing and solving violence – many other forces play crucial roles. However, research and education are important components in lowering the risk of violence and in increasing the chances for the design of more effective peace support strategies. All societies are more or less violent: however, the key to peace and fruitful progress is to manage conflict peacefully. Particularly in societies that have experienced, or still are experiencing, persistent levels of violence – such as the many societies plagued by protracted social conflict – will have to transform their cultures of violence into cultures of peace. This is of course easier said than done and requires a very long-term perspective. Not only will political, economic, and cultural institutions have to be built and rebuilt, but creating a culture of peace entails a social engineering process that requires a massive (re)educational process. Enemy images have to be dismantled, and confidence within society has to be generated (Blagescu, 2004).

Research supports the creation and strengthening of institutions and structures that facilitate peaceful conflict management. Research assists in risk assessment, early warning, and the design of early response strategies, and it assesses and monitors the responses launched by states and international organizations. If well understood and utilized, there are opportunities for analysts to provide and recommend solutions to suitable actors who are in a position to initiate change.[7]

Thorough research can generate the knowledge that is necessary to use available resources wisely and meaningfully, and to address the most critical root causes of violence at the right entry point and time and by the most adequate actor. Research must be conducted internally, externally, and between those two levels, and it must feed into proper channels of communication to reach the potential intervener in an evolving or actual conflict situation.

Scarce resources have to be pooled, coordinated and maximized. Research should be conducted not only for its own sake, but also for the sake of policy change. Results should reach as many stakeholders as possible. Ideally, this should be done in a coordinated fashion:

- *Locally*: by local centres of excellence, and interdisciplinary and dedicated peace research institutions at universities.
- *Nationally*: by national centres of excellence, through nationwide cooperation, and input into government work.
- *Regionally*: by regional centres of excellence, through region-wide cooperation, and input into government work (I will return to the potential roles of such centres later in this chapter).
- *Globally*: through global conferences, and input into UN, World Bank, and IMF programmes, and the wider donor/assistance community.
- *Field work*: by conducting country reports, systematic monitoring, and effective sharing of research results.

While research in its own right possesses its intrinsic value and justification, research about violent societies bears a sense of responsibility for the research environment – the respondent and his or her life conditions. There is an ethical responsibility to put research results to productive use in improving the situation for the research respondents.

Ethical issues and responsibility towards the researched population

Research in – and about – violent societies should at least attempt to be impact-oriented. This is not to say that all research is required to have an applied policy focus, yet at least an honest attempt should be made to turn some component of the research effort into positive effects for the researched population. This can be achieved by influencing local decision-makers and their policies, or international actors (government agencies, international and regional organizations, or intergovernmental organizations) operating in a conflictive society. However, often this is not done. Once researchers return from the field, they quickly forget the expectations raised and promises made while working with their respondents; they are preoccupied with writing up their research results, with the search for academically profitable publication venues, and with securing new financial research grants. Unless donors require and fund activities to bring research results back to the field, this often does not happen. Moreover, little academic credit tends to be granted to applied policy work. Once the results are published, it is assumed to be the task of others to apply these findings in some form or another. The danger of becoming entirely detached from the research theatre may be less pertinent for projects by policy-oriented research institutes or think tanks with operational field presence and/or specific capacity-building mandates. Although still strong in academic rigour, their output often is more diverse than in university and research environments, focusing on both academic contributions and – if appropriate and useful – field applications of their findings and recommendations.

During the meeting of authors for this book, the project participants and additional attendees from the University of Ibadan, Nigeria, and other local institutions met for a workshop on ethical protection of social science research in violently divided societies. The workshop generated a number of observations and recommendations about the role of internal and external researchers in violently divided societies, with an emphasis on Africa (Smyth, 2002).[8] Three main themes and concerns became apparent: unethical behaviour in the generation of data; ethical issues related to ownership and implementation of research results; and safety issues for both local and external researchers. On the first issue, there is concern about the use of data that has been faked by researchers, and the provision of and reference to unreliable data produced by governments and other agencies. Financial limitations and pressure to produce tangible research results may tempt some researchers to fabricate or use fake data. For instance, the practice of some academics to use students as both researchers and respondents, also in apparent attempts to limit costs and effort, clearly comes at the expense of quality and validity of research results.

The second concern relates to ethical issues regarding the ownership of research results and the right or responsibility to ensure that results are disseminated to relevant target audiences. When research is produced with data that has been collected from local respondents, the respondents have a stake in the results. They should be considered the true owners of the data, which is held in trust (but not owned) by the researcher. As a consequence, respondents should at a minimum be offered the right to access published research results and the opportunity to use, respond, and challenge the analysis and interpretations of those results. Otherwise, the artificial division between the passive research "object" (the researched population) and the active researcher creates a non-participatory, closed, and imbalanced approach towards advancing knowledge and understanding on issues of crucial concern to the former. Such exclusion may also lead to disillusionment and respondent fatigue. This particularly applies to cases where external researchers seem to appropriate their respondents' ideas and locally-created research results and fail to attribute them to their original sources, presenting them to their community and target audiences as their own findings. This discourages local researchers from collaborating with external researchers, and it undermines the potential benefits from research partnerships and synergies.

Such asymmetric relationships are counter-productive, as researchers from the North, who tend to be at an advantage when it comes to the means to conduct research in southern countries, need to collaborate with partners in the field. The degree to which research can be undertaken without partnerships depends on the degree and time that researchers have been exposed to the location of their study, on their knowledge of the local language, cultural competence, and socio-historical and other relevant knowledge. It should not come as a surprise that those with the most thorough understanding of the local context are also likely to be most appreciative of close collaboration with local partners, and vice versa. Such partnerships must avoid counter-productive and inappropriate, but nevertheless often-displayed, arrogance on the part of the Northern researcher, and should be based on mutual respect and appreciation of each other's strengths and limitations. Such mutual respect is crucial to the aims of this book. This dynamic also occasionally applies to diaspora researchers – indigenous researchers who have been trained in the North, are living and working there as area specialists and occasionally return to their home communities for data collection. However, more so than in the case of Northern researchers, they may be expected by local colleagues to "give back" to their communities, contribute to building local capacity, and assist in knowledge generation. They must ensure that researching violent societies is not simply a one-way affair: publications and recognition for the researcher back home must in some way translate into benefits for the researched population, even if only by sharing one's analysis with partners and respondents on the ground (Smyth, 2001: 5).

The gathering in Ibadan raised a related, yet sometimes delicate, issue: it is clear that some areas are over-researched, in part due to the availability of disproportional research funds and/or a donor's strategic or cultural interests in a particular society. In these cases, researched communities realize that researchers are not necessarily motivated by the desire to generate new insights, or to be of assistance to the affected society, but that they are guided by professional ambitions and the availability of research funds, rather than by research needs. In such situations, there is little incentive for research populations to contribute to such projects. In the absence of unlimited funding sources, concentration of research funds and efforts (for instance, on Northern Ireland or the Balkans, in comparison to most conflict regions on the African continent) translates into disproportionally meagre availability of funds for research and in turn into strategically less "significant", yet often more disastrous, conflicts elsewhere in the world. Research on and in Africa continues to suffer from this dynamic despite efforts of some organizations, including the UN, to assure that greater attention is given within the global research community to African needs.

A further, related concern regards the position of the researcher towards the role of violence in social and state–society interaction. Some researchers entirely reject violence as a means towards political change, while many Africans consider violence to be the only language that corrupt governments or companies understand. For instance, local communities in the Niger Delta confront oil companies with the help of paramilitary groups. Support for such actions is considered a legitimate and effective means of communication, as well as a source of community pride. Yet, some researchers may reject and disregard the voice of these local communities. Remuneration (including financial compensation or the provision of goods and material) of respondents for their services presents another delicate issue. On the one hand, the services and needs of communities should be recognized, yet payment might distort the respondents' responses – they might deliver whatever the researchers want to hear, and not what they need to hear. Finally, both researchers and respondents need to understand the purpose of the research, and they need to be able to focus on a comprehensive analysis of the collected data rather than on particular factors that may serve the researchers' professional needs, but cannot offer useful results for the consumption and consideration of the respondents and their communities.

Finally, as noted also by Smyth in the previous chapter, the security of both researchers and their subjects may be at stake during research activities in societies marked by violence. On the one hand, researchers have the responsibility to protect the rights of their research subjects, while they also have to be concerned about their own – and their staff's – safety in a volatile context. Both dimensions should be better reflected in ethical codes of conduct, research methods, and ethics literature. Once research results are published, potentially negative – and dangerous – results must be anticipated. Both researchers and their partners and respondents might be threatened by certain parties after publication of the research results. Researchers have the responsibility to anticipate such threats against themselves and their respondents. This is all the more important when the anonymity of the respondents is crucial to their safety – all potentially compromising information that could identify the respondents must be excluded from any published text, even if such omissions would weaken the scientific value of the researcher's evidence and arguments. Furthermore, particularly in post-conflict societies, researchers should understand and must take into consideration the negative effect that research into traumatization, or with traumatized populations, might have on the respondents and the researcher alike.

In summary, the workshop held at the University of Ibadan, Nigeria, has made it abundantly clear that conducting research in violent societies entails a wide array of responsibilities, which require thorough preparation and precautionary strategies by both researchers and respondents. Expectations run high among respondents that research results, generated by internal and external researchers, will produce improvements. Often there will not be a return on their investment – that is, the time, effort and, occasionally, danger associated with the participation in a research project on highly delicate political issues. Two factors, among others, seem to be at the root of often disappointing returns on local input in research on violence. First, even the most significant and potentially path-breaking and relevant research results remain non- or under-utilized if the researcher fails to present them to relevant policy audiences. Reasons for such failure may be lack of motivation on the part of the researcher to get involved in the implementation of his or her own research results. Researchers might not be interested in widening their target audience to include decision-makers who have the ability to apply the practical lessons of their research results. Even if researchers include decision-makers in their circle of target audiences (or even declare them as their primary targets), they might not succeed in their efforts if they fail to "reach" their target audience with a product that has been inadequately prepared and delivered for policy and practitioner consumption. The following section will be devoted to this dilemma. Second, particularly well-funded and, thus, well-documented research into violent societies is often dominated by external projects, funding and researchers, while local, national and regional potentials for quality research remain dormant due to a lack of funding, opportunity and capacities for locally-generated research. That issue will be addressed in the form of several recommendations towards the end of this chapter.

Impact and influence on decision-makers

Beyond the social engineering component of (preventive) peace education, the leap from research to effective early warning and prevention requires researchers to transfer their findings to those individuals and institutions who have the means and opportunities to translate research findings and recommendations into actual policies. Research results have to reach decision-makers or those analysts who work in the offices of local and national governments, and of intergovernmental organizations. Yet, often this leap is not being accomplished and valuable research results do not find their way into the hands, documents, and arguments of policy-makers and their immediate advisors. Given what is at stake, the inability to share one's research findings (often generated at great effort and risk, as discussed in the previous section) is negligent – and represents a breach of trust towards those who are led to believe that their participation in a research project will result in improvements for them and their communities.

Two main reasons are responsible for this failure to attract greater attention from decision- and policy-makers. On the one hand, research themes often do not correspond to policy needs (or they are only marginally related), or are too academic in nature and offer few or no policy options. On the other hand, they are often not presented in an effective, user-friendly way to relevant target audiences.

An INCORE study has addressed the link between research and policy in the context of a number of international organizations (Williams and Robinson, 1999). The study found that policy-makers tend to have too little time to do their own research, consult research done by others, or even to reflect on their own practice and experience. They are tied up with emergency situations, particularly if dealing with or working in conflict regions. Moreover, they often experience great changes and shifts in their duties and responsibilities, which are inconstant movement between and among pre-conflict, conflict, and post-conflict stages along the conflict spectrum. As a consequence, there are no straightforward questions that could be answered with straightforward responses, nor is there much time to research solutions to problems of immediate concern. On the other hand, the study argues that continuously changing responsibilities and challenges force policy-makers and their staff to appreciate flexible, new approaches – new answers to perhaps old problems, which could be provided by innovative research.

This INCORE study found that research is more likely to influence policy if it meets the following requirements: it has to be generalizable, crossing geographical lines, disciplines, and situations; it has to cover long-term consequences of policy and practice; it is undertaken and presented by a known and credible person; it addresses real problems of international agencies; it is presented in a provocative, focused, concise, and timely manner; it addresses the research topic from a variety of perspectives; it raises the level of policy debate through the introduction of new concepts and frameworks; it either supports existing thinking of policy-makers or challenges them with a new paradigm; it must be based on rigorous field research; and it presents a range of policy options (Williams and Robinson, 1999: 9). The latter point is particularly important when working in violent contexts with inter-ethnic divides as in the African focus of this book. There is no room for subjectivity, let alone advocacy, of one or the other conflict side's causes. Research approaches and methodologies, research results, and (policy) recommendations have to be based on facts and thoroughly researched knowledge and data. Otherwise the results appear biased, thus of little value and, at worst, serve to exacerbate existing tensions between conflicting parties.

Research also becomes more influential if policy-makers are involved in the research process, and if their concerns and questions are incorporated into the planning stage, thus creating a sense of shared ownership. Researchers and their institutions should attempt to create platforms for policy-makers to exchange their opinions, concerns and research needs, as well as training opportunities to familiarize policy-makers and their staff with state of the art knowledge on key issues of conflict management (Williams and Robinson, 1999: 10). A further, quite intriguing, observation concerned researchers' unwillingness to draw conclusions based on unfinished or incomplete research, to make projections that go beyond the – often narrow – empirical evidence of their research work, or to generate policy options even from completed research. Decision-makers frequently have to make far-reaching decisions based on incomplete information, far below the threshold of what researchers would consider adequate evidence. Researchers must learn how to balance rigorous quality research with the timely and policy-relevant communication of research results. They have to learn how to act more like expert consultants – they must be in a position to translate their findings into recommendations and options for policy generation (Williams and Robinson, 1999: 10).

As already pointed out above, a further weakness is the researchers' inability to present their findings in a user-friendly way. As mentioned in an earlier section of this chapter, researchers owe it to those researched that their efforts reach the ears and thoughts of those individuals and organizations that may be in a position to translate research results into improvements on the ground. What are some of the suggestions made by policy-makers themselves to improve the "packaging" and effective presentation of research results, thus improving the impact of research efforts? For written outputs, professionals note that *influential* research is presented in brief, concise, digestible, and readable formats. Recommendations for action include suggestions for evaluations, including impact indicators. They avoid overly academic language and "speak" to the target audience. They offer policy options, even contradictory ones. Policy-makers are grateful to be offered a range of options, from which they can pick the most suitable one.

While large conference proceedings are not useful, short extractions with the most important information and lessons may well be of use. Oral presentations of research results (often the only way to share one's findings with a practitioner audience that has little or no time to read even the most concise policy briefs), should ideally be informal, engage the audience in discussions, and offer the opportunity for individuals to participate in their non-official capacity. This could be a lunchtime series or even a large convention – as long as the target persons are away from their offices, telephones, and computer screens. This allows them to free their minds for new ideas and innovative suggestions and approaches. Large official conferences (such as summits of the UN or regional organizations) can also be useful as they produce official communiqués. If they refer to important research findings or policy recommendations, chances are that those ideas are communicated and shared with a larger official audience of decision-making agencies and individuals beyond the occasional individual who may have attended such a meeting.[9]

Again, the most important issue is to get one's results onto the "radar screen" of those who are in a position to utilize one's findings and recommendations. Only then can research be carried beyond a small circle of researchers to those who could possibly implement some of the findings generated through the efforts of researchers, their various partners and donors, and affected respondents and their communities on the ground.

However, for many researchers it is not easy to follow these suggestions as they require time, effort, and money. Many research projects have little or no funding specifically designated for dissemination activities or the preparation of policy briefs. As can be seen from the above discussion, both require considerable effort, capacity, and expertise. If research is to be impact-oriented, its budget must include funds for such activities, and donors must provide for such investment in research-driven and informed policy-making. Donors (or in the case of Southern researchers, their Northern partners) may also consider the provision of educational skill-enhancement opportunities to train researchers in the generation of policy-relevant and impact-oriented dissemination skills. Moreover, researchers need to receive professional credit for these efforts, and – particularly in closed and violent societies – they must be protected by their institutions, partners and donors in cases where their research (and relevant dissemination activities) might expose them to pressure and harassment from government authorities or other groups that stand to lose from the implementation of specific research results and recommendations.

Regional centres of excellence: facilitation of research, provisions of training, and policy advice

Beyond strengthening existing research capacities, fostering new partnerships, and advancing the policy relevance of research into conflictive societies, a number of steps must be taken to advance the improvement of the input of academic research in effective peace support strategies.[10]

The generation of risk and conflict analysis must be improved. In general terms, this is an issue of funding, support for local talent and, in particular, local initiatives. The coordination of analysis must be improved. This requires – more than on merely symbolic, occasional, and ad hoc levels – task-sharing between different institutions and stakeholders and the pooling of resources across local, national, regional, and international levels.[11] The transfer of relevant analysis to suitable response mechanisms must be improved – at nonstate, state and interstate levels. Prescriptive work must be targeted at policy communities. Reflective work must monitor (and feed the results back into) state, nonstate and interstate activities across the entire peace support continuum: before, during, and after violence.

These tasks can be accomplished through the work of regional centres of excellence for research and teaching on such subjects as risk assessment and conflict transformation. Regional centres of excellence should grow out of existing regional centres or national institutes with potentially regional reach; they should integrate or build upon already existing networks; and they should be supported by contributions from universities and research institutions abroad. Such regional centres are urgently needed in Africa, both on a continent-wide basis (possibly under the sponsorship of the Organization of African Unity) as well as in the context of subregions, including sub-Saharan and Southern Africa, the Great Lakes region and the Horn of Africa (also possibly sponsored by subregional organizations) (Smith, 2001). Similar regional centres should also be created in other conflict-prone regions, such as South/Southeast Asia and Latin America. Much can be learned from the Central European University's and the Open Society Fund's experiences in Central/Eastern European and the states of the former Soviet Union.[12] The current focus of international organizations and the wider donor community on strengthening civil society and track two and three activities in conflict-prone regions should be harnessed to strengthen research networks and address previously under-studied or altogether avoided research topics.

To return once more to Osaghae's analysis of the state of research in Africa, some improvement can be noticed,

due to the incorporation of conflict management into the agenda of the donor community to which many governments are beholden. One of the positive results of this has been the influx of international NGOs whose humanitarian activities of necessity include conflict resolution and peacemaking. This has been accompanied by the emergence of local independent research and activist NGOs funded by foreign donors. With so much going on, African governments, especially those embroiled in severe crises and protracted wars, can no longer afford to ignore research findings and the recommendations based on them (Osaghae, 2001: 25–26).

Of course, such efforts have to move beyond the level of externally sponsored "projects" and become self-sustaining. Local and regional networks and centres of excellence have to advance beyond representing initiatives of international donors and NGOs, a maturation and solidification process that applies to civil society in general.[13]

Regional centres of excellence must develop into indispensable assets for civil society and the state to stem the tide of protracted conflict and violence. Based on capacity and expertise, a number of core activities should be offered by such centres. These include the following:

- *Research*: Joint research projects – among network partners and international partners, both from the North and other Southern-based institutions – should address the early indication and resolution of root-causes of violence and injustice. Research should follow ethical standards and commitments to feed results into policy debates at local to international levels of governance, education, and opinion-formation.
- *Publication, dissemination, and evaluation*: For the purpose of timely

production, research results should be published in the first instance as in-house publications in international as well as in local languages. International partners should attempt to feed the results into global debates through publication in major journals or with well-placed book publishers. If at all possible, electronic media such as the internet should be utilized to disseminate preliminary and final research results. As discussed above, effective dissemination strategies (in print and word), and relevant funding for such strategies, should be incorporated into projects at the planning stage. This applies also for evaluation strategies. If at all possible (a common requirement by many donors), the implementation and impact of research and educational projects should be evaluated against specific impact indicators. The latter must be realistic, and the findings must be used for constructive improvements of research and dissemination efforts.

- *Teaching*: Depending on the size and nature of an institution, longer-term academic degree programmes, short 10–12 months' intensive post-graduate programmes, or multi-week certificate programmes may be offered to junior academics and government and NGO practitioners. Ideally, such programmes should include participation from all of those groups, and be offered as joint activities between local and regional institutions, and between local institutions and institutions from abroad. Lessons learned from past and existing collaborative efforts should guide such initiatives.

- *Training*: As part of their dissemination mandate, regional centres of excellence should offer training programmes and workshops for media representatives, educators, NGO workers, and staff of local, national, regional, and UN offices, organized in collaboration with international organizations and capacity-building NGOs. Practitioners are not usually given the time and opportunity to attend academic programmes that last months or years, either on a full- or on a part-time basis. They might, however, be able to attend short training courses or workshops that last anywhere from one to five days. Such courses can be offered to each target audience individually and/or to mixed groups. As an added advantage, mixed groups offer opportunities for exchanges and mutual learning between different groups of actors and stakeholders.

- *Policy Advice*: In consideration of the requirements for effective policy advice, regional centres of excellence should serve as clearing-houses for local, national, and regional experts; formation of expert groups on particular pressing issues; and the production of policy papers and updates for local, regional and national governments (and NGOs).

- *Networking*: Regional centres of excellence should serve as platforms and clearing houses for local and regional talent.

- *Quality and Ethical Control*: Finally, regional centres of excellence should ensure that their network partners (and members of educational and research communities) meet minimum quality and ethical requirements. This includes, among others, the various concerns examined during the Ibadan workshop on conducting ethical research discussed above. At a minimum, "do no harm" control mechanisms (conducted by regional centres) must assure that they do not, willingly or unwillingly, advance violent agendas or otherwise contribute to conflict escalation. The regional centres must serve as the conscience of the community of constructive and ethical research and research partnerships.

The costs for these activities (including overheads, salaries, project costs, honoraria, travel or student fellowships) will generally have to be born primarily by external actors, while some funding has to come from other regional universities (for example, through in-kind, no-cost faculty exchanges). These include institutions abroad, large international foundations, and interested governments.

The activities have to target significant numbers of stakeholders from civil society, academia, and policy communities. Small-scale programmes with little, or merely symbolic, impact must be pooled, bundled, and conducted in a more coordinated and impact-oriented fashion.

Conclusion

In summary, knowledge and understanding of the dynamics and context of potential violence is a crucial key factor at all stages of the violence prevention and conflict management continuum – for proper recognition, timely warning, and adequate response. Research and education within violently divided societies, as well as by those external organizations and societies that would likely intervene at some point along the conflict cycle, is crucial in limiting violent conflict and designing and implementing proper response strategies.

Researchers can play crucial roles in bridging the frequent wide gaps between academics and practitioners, between analysis and policy, and between early recognition, warning, and response. It should be considered a wise investment to strengthen the peacemaking roles and capacities of educational and research institutions in divided, fragile, and transitional societies. This will increase the capacity of local societies and their governments to manage conflicts peacefully, and it will equip external actors to offer adequate, meaningful, and constructive assistance. Only then can we hope for sustainable peace support strategies.

As has been argued in this chapter, researchers and their donors (both local and external) have the ethical responsibility to design and implement projects in such ways that local partners are not put in undue danger and risk. They should be expected to make every effort to use their research to facilitate an improvement of conditions for the researched population. This usually means that the results are fed effectively into policy debates at local, national, regional and/or international levels. Moreover, research capacities in conflict regions must be strengthened, particularly via regional centres of excellence. Africa stands to benefit greatly from such initiatives of giving research a more central role in understanding and overcoming ethnic and other divisions, roots and dynamics of conflict, and in developing mitigation and resolution strategies to avoid and end violent conflict.

Notes

1. For extensive analyses of opportunities and difficulties of preventive action in various regions around the world and by various nonstate, state, and interstate actors, see the two-volume series entitled *Conflict Prevention from Rhetoric to Reality* (Schnabel and Carment, 2004). For examinations of the African context, see Shiawl-Kidanekal (2004), Karuru (2004) and Draman (2003).
2. For a recent contribution to the debate on humanitarian intervention, as well as an excellent and extensive bibliography on recent academic work covering all stages of the conflict cycle, see the International Commission on Intervention and State Sovereignty (2001).
3. For an illustration of the conflict cycle, and possible response strategies, see Lund (1996: 38).
4. For helpful analyses of intergovernmental, subregional, and civil society actors' roles in preventing and managing African conflicts, see Parlevliet (2001), Schnabel (2001), Smith (2001), and Solomon (2001).
5. These three tracks refer to official government (Track One), unofficial non-government (Track Two), and grassroots (Track Three) actors. The unofficial track can be further broken down – for instance, the Institute for Multi-Track Diplomacy speaks of one official and eight unofficial tracks. In that scheme Track Five is devoted to actors in "research, training, and education", see the Institute for Multi-Track Diplomacy: http://www.imtd.org/about-theory.htm.
6. Although the record is poor – mostly for lack of substantial local and international political will and capacity – there is new impetus from and within the UN (the Executive Office of the Secretary-General, the United Nations Department of Political Affairs, the United Nations System Staff College), the World Bank and IMF, and regional organizations and NGOs that are more receptive and socially responsible.
7. See, for instance, the methodology and products of the early warning programme FAST of swisspeace, Bern. See http://www.swisspeace.org/fast/default.htm.
8. The following discussion draws on Marie Smyth's report of the workshop discussions.
9. The suggestions referred to in this paragraph draw in part on the findings of Williams and Robinson (1999).
10. An example of an innovative North–South effort to strengthen research capacity within Southern research hubs, and Northern and Southern institutions through

network-building and support of young academics is the Swiss National Centre for Competence in Research (NCCR) North-South, see www.nccr-north-south.unibe.ch.
11. Such associations could draw loosely on the work of the European Platform for Conflict Prevention and Transformation, see http://www.euconflict.org/.
12. See the Central European University: http://www.ceu.hu/.
13. For a discussion of civil society's contributions, see Parlevliet (2001).

REFERENCES

Baker, Pauline H. and Ausink, John A. (1996) "State Collapse and Ethnic Violence: Toward a Predictive Model", *Parameters* 26(1): 19–36.

Ball, Nicole (1996) "The Challenge of Rebuilding War-Torn Societies", in Chester A. Crocker, Fen Osler Hampson with Pamela Aall, eds., *Managing Global Chaos: Sources of and Responses to International Conflict*, Washington, DC: United States Institute of Peace Press, pp. 608–612.

Blagescu, Monica (2004) "Conflict Prevention through Peace Education: A Debate", in David Carment and Albrecht Schnabel, eds., *Conflict Prevention from Rhetoric to Reality: Opportunities and Innovations*, Lanham, MD.: Lexington Books, pp. 199–226.

Carment, David and Schnabel, Albrecht, eds. (2003) *Conflict Prevention: Path to Peace or Grand Illusion?*, Tokyo: United Nations University Press, pp. 233–253.

——— (2004) *Conflict Prevention from Rhetoric to Reality: Opportunities and Innovations*, Lanham, MD.: Lexington Books.

Carnegie Commission on Preventing Deadly Conflict (1997) *Preventing Deadly Conflict*, Final Report, New York: Carnegie Corporation of New York.

Draman, Rasheed (2003) "Conflict Prevention in Africa: Establishing Conditions and Institutions Conducive to Durable Peace", in David Carment and Albrecht Schnabel, eds., *Conflict Prevention: Path to Peace or Grand Illusion?*, Tokyo: United Nations University Press, pp. 233–253.

Esty, Daniel C., Goldstone, Jack A., Gurr, Ted Robert, Surko, Pamela T., and Unger, Alan N. (1995) *Working Paper: State Failure Task Force Report*, 30 November.

International Commission on Intervention and State Sovereignty (2001) *The Responsibility to Protect, Report of the International Commission on Intervention and State Sovereignty*, Ottawa: International Development Research Centre.

Karuru, Njeri (2004) "Conflict Prevention: Responses by Subregional Organizations and Civil Society Organizations in Eastern Africa", in Albrecht Schnabel and David Carment, eds., *Conflict Prevention from Rhetoric to Reality: Organizations and Institutions*, Lanham, MD.: Lexington Books, pp. 263–285.

Lund, Michael (1996) *Preventing Violent Conflict: A Strategy for Preventive Diplomacy*, Washington DC: United States Institute of Peace Press.

Osaghae, Eghosa E. (2001) "The Role and Function of Research in Divided Societies: The Case of Africa", in Marie Smyth and Gillian Robinson, eds., *Researching Violently Divided Societies: Ethical and Methodological Issues*, London: Pluto Press/Tokyo: United Nations University Press, pp. 12–33.

Parlevliet, Michelle (2001) "Containment or Change? Civil Society's Role in Conflict Prevention in Africa", in Elizabeth Sidiropoulos, ed., *A Continent Apart: Kosovo, Africa and Humanitarian Intervention*, Johannesburg: South African Institute of International Affairs, pp. 61–88.

Schnabel, Albrecht (2001) "Preventing Wars within States: What can Intergovernmental Organizations do in Africa?", in Elizabeth Sidiropoulos, ed., *A Continent Apart: Kosovo, Africa and Humanitarian Intervention*, Johannesburg: South African Institute of International Affairs, pp. 13–36.

——— (2002) "Post-Conflict Peacebuilding and Second-Generation Preventive Action", *International Peacekeeping* 9(2): 24–25.

——— (2003) "Democratization and Peacebuilding", in Amin Saikal and Albrecht Schnabel, eds., *Democratization in the Middle East: Experiences, Struggles, Challenges*, Tokyo: United Nations University Press, pp. 25–41.

Schnabel, Albrecht and David Carment, eds., (2004) *Conflict Prevention from Rhetoric to Reality: Organizations and Institutions*, Lanham, MD.: Lexington Books.

Shiawl-Kidanekal, Teferra (2004) "Conflict Prevention and Management in Africa", in Albrecht Schnabel and David Carment, eds., *Conflict Prevention from Rhetoric to Reality: Organizations and Institutions*, Lanham, MD.: Lexington Books, pp. 149–163.

Smith, Betsie (2001) "The Role of Subregional and Regional Organizations in Preventing African Conflicts", in Elizabeth Sidiropoulos, ed., *A Continent Apart: Kosovo, Africa and Humanitarian Intervention*, Johannesburg: South African Institute of International Affairs, pp. 37–59.

Smyth, Marie (2001) "Introduction", in Marie Smyth and Gillian Robinson, eds., *Researching Violently Divided Societies: Ethical and Methodological Issues*, London: Pluto Press/Tokyo: United Nations University Press, pp. 1–11.

——— (2002) "Report from workshop on a review of ethics in the social sciences", Derry/Londonderry: INCORE, May.

Solomon, Hussein (2001) "The Role of Civil Society in Reconstruction, Rehabilitation and Reconciliation in Africa", in Elizabeth Sidiropoulos, ed., *A Continent Apart: Kosovo, Africa and Humanitarian Intervention*, Johannesburg: South African Institute of International Affairs, pp. 243–255.

Williams, Sue and Robinson, Gillian (1999) "Research and Policy: An INCORE consultative review of research processes, research priorities and the usefulness of research to policy-makers at the United Nations and other international organizations", Derry/Londonderry: INCORE.

II

Researching ethnic conflict
and violent division:
African case studies

3

The role and function of research in a divided society: A case study of the Niger-Delta region of Nigeria

Bolanle Akande Adetoun

The 1990s witnessed an upsurge of violent conflicts in various parts of Nigeria, particularly in the Niger-Delta region. The Niger-Delta is the most reported and talked about region in Nigeria today as a result of being enmeshed in different types of communal conflicts which often have erupted into mass violence. Located in the south of the country around the tributaries of River Niger, the Niger-Delta covers an area of 70,000 kilometres, consists of the nine states of Rivers, Delta, Abia, Bayelsa, Cross-Rivers, Akwa-Ibom, Ondo, Imo, and Edo and has an estimated population of about nine million. The region consists of the majority of the southern ethnic minorities (such as the Ijaw, Urhobo, Ogoni, Ilaje and Itsekiri) and it is where Nigeria derives the crude petroleum oil that is the country's economic lifeline.

The Niger-Delta crisis first reared its head in 1965, when the late Isaac Boro and his group took up arms to fight for a separate nation for the region. Though more restive after 1965, the situation reached boiling point in 1990 when the region's elite and its youth formed various organizations to protest against the marginalization, neglect, oppression, and exploitation of their people and resources. Since 1990, the crisis has been violent and militant, often resulting in the loss of human lives and properties. The violence continues and, in 2003, about one hundred people were killed and a thousand people injured because of this conflict.

The Niger-Delta crisis is a complex one, with each of the region's ethnic groups fighting its neighbours. They are seemingly all enemies, with no two groups being able to unite in friendship. Indeed, the groups can be seen to have assumed the status of social movements, since the various groups have organized themselves into associations for protesting against their perceived marginalization. In addition, other issues further complicate the situation. For example, the ethnic groups are not only fighting each other, but seem to be waging an undeclared war on the Nigerian state. Additionally, they have disputes against the multinational oil companies. This adds another dimension of taking the conflicts into the international arena, beyond Nigerian borders and citizens.

These characteristics qualify the Niger-Delta as a divided society. The central question I address in this chapter is what role social science research plays in such a society, and I explore this with pertinent examples from my research on "ethnic conflict and socio-economic development in the Niger-Delta Region of Nigeria".[1] Lack of development has been at the core of the various conflicts in the Niger-Delta, with many issues concerning access to resources and fairness in resource sharing. A number of responses from governmental and non-governmental agencies (especially the multinational oil companies) have been geared both directly and indirectly to the improved socio-economic development of the area through various projects and programmes, but the paradox is that the provision of such developmental assistance also generates substantial intra- and inter-ethnic conflict. The cumulative effect is that when two steps are taken forwards towards the socio-economic development of the region, ethnic conflicts ensure that one step is taken back. Conflict analysis, prevention, and resolution therefore need to be a central dimension in socio-economic developmental planning and implementation in the Niger-Delta.

The role of research and researchers in a divided society

Objectivity and impartiality

First, in a divided society, the researcher must be someone who will strive for impartiality and be unbiased in his or her analysis. With this in mind, I think it unlikely that a member of one of the conflicting groups would be able to conduct scientific research, as they are usually too emotionally involved in the various issues and would tend to work from a subjective perspective. Indeed, I believe that in most cases, such people are involved in propaganda – a look at the various websites set up by the different ethnic groups is persuasive of this fact. A good example is the issue of who owns Warri, one of the big cities in the region. This has been one of the most contentious issues in the Niger-Delta. Three ethnic groups (Urhobo, Ijaw, and Itsekiri) that are all trying to dominate local politics, currently lay claim to being the indigenous and native people of Warri. The groups have each set up various means (including websites) of communicating and defending their ethnic position, and their various accounts of "indigenousness" are conflicting and contradictory.[2] Each has engaged in some propaganda and subjectivity in their analysis – none of the research presented by these groups appears to have been undertaken with the key scientific principles of unbiased and impartial research in mind. Thus the role of a researcher into conflict in the Niger-Delta is to strive towards objectivity, to give an impartial analysis of the various issues, and to make their findings available to all stakeholders and policy-makers, in the hope of leading to better policy formulation and implementation.

It is vital for researchers to protect the identity of their respondents in order not to expose them to any kind of recrimination from opposing groups – the researcher must not precipitate further crisis. The purpose of the research should be explained to all interviewees, and it should be made clear that all responses will be kept strictly confidential and the identity of individuals will not be disclosed (other than any that have been made public via television programmes, newspaper reports, court proceedings and so forth).

Methodologies

The researcher should be well-versed in the various tools of the trade, and as a social scientist, should be willing to see which appropriate interdisciplinary tools can be further utilized. A sociologist, for example, might use the anthropological methodologies of ethnographic studies and focused group discussions. The researcher should proceed systematically using the proper sample design bearing in mind the issues of representativeness, validity, and reliability. In my own study, for example, I planned to interview all the major stakeholders in the conflict, such as community leaders and members, government policy-makers and implementers (Niger-Delta Development Commission officers and local government officers), representatives of the multinational oil companies and, since my focus is on the Warri region, members of the three "indigenous" ethnic groups in conflict over the city. The data for my study came from both these primary sources and from secondary sources such as newspapers, magazines, government publications, community publications, and memoranda.

My intention was to conduct two sets of interviews: one for the development agencies (such as government agencies and oil companies) and other stakeholders; and the other for the community members and leaders – the project beneficiaries. I also used the socio-anthropological method of focused group discussions with small groups of stakeholders with the aim of generating knowledge of the socio-cultural realities that heightened the conflicts in the development programmes. Before any interviews and discussions, however, I gathered as much information as I could from the various publications and spoke to people from the region who are now resident outside it. With this varied knowledge, I was able to lead the discussions appropriately during the sets of interviews and to ask for valuable expansion and clarification on various issues as needed.

Information, knowledge, and analysis

I believe the work of a researcher in this type of project is to listen to all parties concerned and then to analyse the findings with regard to the basic issues of convergence and divergence. For instance, the underlying factor to most of these crises is poverty, both absolute and relative. Many people in the Niger-Delta lack the basic necessities for a decent living, and there is a high level of youth unemployment. Highly visible alongside this abject poverty is the opulent lifestyle of the oil company workers and the developments of infrastructure in various other parts of the country, all accomplished from the oil wealth derived from their Niger-Delta region. Thus, the main factor fuelling the conflicts in the area concerns the nature of the Nigerian state and how far it has been able to meet the socio-economic rights of the people of the region.

The study of the conflict, its resolution and prevention therefore has two main concerns. First, it is necessary to offer an explanation of the issues involved in the conflict and violence. It is only on the basis of an adequate explanation of a problem that we can evolve constructive approaches to solving it. After an explanation of the problem of conflict is given, the second concern is to find the nature of a constructive approach to the problem, thereby outlining the principles, processes, and policies that can be derived from the explanation (Burton, 1990).

My study, for example, has been able to identify some of the under-lying issues that seem to be recurring in the various conflicts involved in the socio-economic development of the Niger-Delta region:

- There are inter- and intra-ethnic/community conflicts over land owner-ship arising from efforts to determine who is entitled to compensation and other benefits from the oil companies.
- The various development projects established actually seem to pro-mote inter-group conflict and rivalry: one group, for example, might feel that a particular company has done much for another group while doing little for them. Thus, the various ethnic groups do make compar-isons of various benefits derived from the same oil company or compare different oil companies.

- There have been conflicts when projects do not satisfy the felt needs of the communities.
- The communities feel that adequate compensations for oil spills and acquisition of farmlands are not being paid to them. The oil companies also have been accused of promoting violence by often inviting the police when any dispute arises from paying compensations or granting indigenous employment quotas.
- As far as the communities are concerned, the oil companies quote high amounts for the cost of projects that do not match what is seen on the ground; neither is there any evidence of their contributions to the people's well-being. Some of the communities also complain that the quality of amenities provided by the oil companies is below the standard for their own personnel or those that the same companies provide elsewhere in the world.
- Some contractors collect contract money but do not execute the projects.
- There are persistent and increasing demands for socio-economic development by host communities from the oil companies.
- Youths of some communities are pitched against their elders, accusing them of duping their communities of various benefits for their own selfish ends.
- Rival youth groups within a community seek to be recognized as authentic representatives of their people and claim diverse benefits from oil companies.

Researchers in this type of project can also undertake ethnographic studies in order to find out the historical narratives of the past and their influence on the present situation. Such ethnographic study can help in identifying commonalities – historical, cultural, religious, and economic which could help to promote sustainable conflict resolution. Furthermore, there has been an increasingly widespread recognition that repeated failure and various conflicts have plagued many development programmes sponsored by national and international agencies in the developing countries. Therefore, these issues have heightened the interest in identifying and addressing the socio-cultural variables that impinge on the success of such projects. In addition, due to the rising public concern for environmental protection, sustainable development, citizen participation, and institution-building, more socio-anthropological knowledge derived from research has been employed to improve the quality and reduce the inherent conflict of development work. Knowledge derived from research therefore has been used systematically as a complement to economic and technical knowledge in order to promote citizen participation and democracy (all of which lessen the inherent conflicts in developmental projects) in planned development interventions (Cernea, 1985).

In order to have peace and sustainable development in the Niger-Delta, various financial investments into the socio-economic development of the area have to recognize adequately prevailing local institutional and social structures. Even though financial resources are indispensable, many internationally assisted development programmes have often failed not because of lack of finance, but due to the inability of the particular society to use finance effectively, or, sometimes, because of the inability of the project planners to design an efficient way for absorbing these new resources. Salient socio-cultural variables continue to impact upon projects; and if these variables are not addressed or are mishandled, irrespective of the heavy financial investments, then the projects will fail and generate further conflicts.

For example, a socio-anthropological study of 57 World Bank-financed projects (Kotak, 1985), which examined the association between the socio-cultural fit (or misfit) of project design and the estimated economic rate of return at project completion (audit) time, found that the attention given to the issues of socio-cultural compatibility paid off significantly in economic terms and in enhancing a peaceful atmosphere for sustainable development. According to Kotak (1985), from his analyses of 18 projects, these tended to be less successful when the project planners and implementers ignored the established socio-economic and cultural patterns. After an extensive review of various projects, Kotak concluded that flexibility, involvement of beneficiaries, drawing on pre-existing social units, and continuous monitoring of local conditions should be part and parcel of sound project implementation strategies. He also asserted that, if poverty alleviation and more equitable income distribution are to be enhanced for current and future development projects, the quality of socio-economic information collected before, during, and after project implementation must be improved. It is through socio-economic and cultural study done during the preparation, monitoring, and evaluation of the project that the culturally specific incentives necessary to obtain and to enhance local participation become apparent.

According to Uphoff (1985), participation in development projects is enhanced when the design and implementation of such projects are tailored to the needs and capabilities of the beneficiaries. In his review of three World Bank Integrated Rural Development assisted projects in Nepal (Asia), Ghana (Africa), and Mexico (Latin America), he found that the projects were less successful than anticipated because the planners did not pay due regard to the experience and ideas of farmers and technicians working in the project area. In addition, all the three projects encountered problems of coordination and delay during their implementation. However, in various ways, the projects have been modified to become more open to people's participation and consequently the results

have been more satisfactory with minimal conflict. It is therefore important and valuable to invest in an initial and continuing knowledge base
through socio-economic research. Thus project design and implementation should reflect a "learning approach" (two-way communication
consisting of a feedback mechanism between the implementers and
beneficiaries), which enlists the participation of the intended beneficiaries
as much as is feasible in all aspects of project operations. This will serve
to lessen the conflict generated as an outcome of developmental assistance (Uphoff, 1985).

As a lot of national and international investment has been (and continues to be) put into Niger-Delta socio-economic development,[3] the
level of effectiveness of these projects and programmes and their impact
on conflict prevention and resolution between and within the communities need to be examined. This is particularly relevant when one
considers the evaluation of Shell Petroleum company projects, which
revealed that only about half the projects were functioning within less
than six years of their commissioning. According to the Community
Relations Manager of Shell Petroleum Development Company (SPDC),
due to increasing and varying demands, the company has increased its
allocation for social and economic infrastructure for the communities
where their operations are based. SPDC expenditure on community
development rose from about US$2 million to about US$32 million in
1997 and to over US$48 million in 1998. The money was spent on such
projects as water, schools, roads, health facilities, youth training schemes,
and support for science teachers to accept postings to rural areas. SPDC
also conducted a survey of those projects completed between 1992 and
1997 and the accountants from KPMG audited the survey. According to
the audited report, 57 per cent of the projects were fully functional while
some 28 per cent were partially functional – meaning they require minor
repairs (Omiyi, 1999). It is therefore pertinent to examine the impact of
these various socio-economic projects, their levels of success and any
constraining factors to their success. Data needs to be gathered to monitor socio-economic conditions and the success of conflict prevention
amongst the Niger-Delta people in order to know the progress being
made and in order to avoid the vicious cycle of neglect and apathy, which
has been fuelling ethnic conflicts in this region. The information
generated from this type of study could be very useful to government
policy-makers and donor agencies involved in international cooperation.

A researcher in this type of study is both contributing to knowledge
and providing material that can be used as a basis for testing scientific
theories. For example, the theory of conflict analysis says that conflicts
can be analysed as to whether external or internal elites or groups trigger
them; domestic elites are often the catalytic factors that turn conflict

situations into violent confrontations. Thus, conflict analysis and prevention efforts should focus on the decisions and actions of domestic elites (Brown, 1997). Undoubtedly, domestic elites have played significant roles in the Niger-Delta region conflict right from the beginning. Many prominent names, for instance, are closely associated with the Warri conflict.

Research in a divided society can also be used in order to understand the perspectives of the different stakeholders on what constitutes sustainable conflict resolution. Thus in my study, one of the last questions discussed in interviews always went thus: "We would like to know from your own perspective what are the strategies for project implementation and operation that are needed to minimize conflicts and to elicit and sustain the beneficiaries' participation in the socio-economic development of the Niger-Delta"? In conducting the research, the researcher also becomes better educated on the various issues involved in the conflict.

In conclusion, I have identified seven key roles for research and the researcher in a divided society. First, the researcher should listen to all parties concerned and find out about different understandings of the conflict in order to analyse the basic issues of convergence and divergence. He or she will then be able to offer an explanation of the issues involved in the conflict and violence. Second, the researcher also can undertake ethnographic studies in order to know the historical narratives of the past and their influence on the present situation. Third, social knowledge derived from research can be used systematically as a complement to economic and technical knowledge in order to promote citizen participation and democracy (all of which lessen the inherent conflicts in developmental projects) in planned development interventions. Fourth, research can provide data to monitor the changes in socio-economic conditions and their impact on conflict prevention amongst the populations of divided societies. Fifth, the researcher contributing to knowledge can use the study as a basis for testing scientific theories and for improved policy planning and implementation. Sixth, research in a divided society can be used in order to understand the perspectives of the different stakeholders on sustainable conflict resolution. Finally, research in a divided society is vital and can make an invaluable contribution to bridging dividing lines when it is properly planned, executed, disseminated and utilized by the relevant stakeholders.

Notes

1. This research has been funded by the Harry Frank Guggenheim Foundation, New York, USA.
2. For the Urhobo sites, see www.waado.org; www.urhobowaado.info; www.urhobo.kinsfolk.com. For the Ijaw site see http://nigerdeltacongress.com. For the Itsekiri site see http://itsurmov.itsekiri.net.

3. One unique aspect of the way in which the Nigerian government has dealt with the Niger-Delta conflict is the setting up of the Oil Mineral Producing Areas Development Commission (OMPADEC) in 1992, a statutory commission to cater for the needs of the oil-producing communities. The Commission received the federal government statutory allocation to mineral-producing states and is charged with using the money for the socio-economic development of the area. OMPADEC has since wound up its activities and has been replaced by the Niger-Delta Development Commission (NDDC), which has the same main goal of improving the socio-economic conditions of the Niger-Delta people. According to Nigerian Vice-President Atiku Abubakar, the NDDC will address "all the socio-economic and ecological problems of the area". The NDDC is therefore the major policy instrument by which the Olusegun Obasanjo government, elected in March 1999 and re-elected in April 2003, intends to intervene in the Niger-Delta in order to reduce ethnic conflict and promote socio-economic development.

REFERENCES

Brown, Michael E. (1997) "The causes of internal conflict: an overview", in Michael E. Brown; Owen R. Coté, Jr.; Sean M. Lynn-Jones; and Steven E. Miller, eds., *Nationalism and Ethnic Conflict*, Massachusetts: MIT Press.

Burgess, Michael (1993) "Federalism and federation: a reappraisal", in Michael Burgess and Alain G. Gagnon, eds., *Comparative Federalism and Federation: Competing Traditions and Future Directions*, Toronto: University of Toronto.

Burton, John (1990) *Conflict: Resolution and Prevention*, Vol. 1, Basingstoke: Macmillan.

Cernea, Michael M., ed. (1985) *Putting People First: Sociological Variables in Rural Development*, New York and London: Oxford University Press for the World Bank.

Kotak, Conrad P. (1985) "When people don't come first: some sociological lessons from completed projects", in Michael M. Cernea, ed., *Putting People First: Sociological Variables in Rural Development*, New York/London: Oxford University Press for World Bank, pp. 431–464.

Omiyi, Basil (1999) "Community relations in the Niger Delta basin", *Post Express Newspaper*, 15 April, Lagos, Nigeria.

Uphoff, Norman (1985) "Fitting projects to people", in Michael M. Cernea, ed., *Putting People First: Sociological Variables in Rural Development*, New York/London: Oxford University Press for World Bank, pp. 467–512.

4

Methodological lessons: Working with Liberian and Togolese refugees in Ghana

Dominic Agyeman

This chapter is an attempt to document the experiences gained in a survey of two refugee camps in Ghana, which were occupied in the early 1990s by refugees from Liberia and Togo. Thousands of refugees arrived from Liberia fleeing political violence, extra-judicial executions and the torture of civilians and opponents by the warring factions that had been involved in the country's civil wars since 1990. Others came from Togo, fleeing violent demonstrations and strikes in support of political reforms and against detentions without trials and extra-judicial executions. At the time the refugees arrived in 1992, Ghana was itself in the process of transformation from a military to a civilian government and therefore was undergoing much political strain and tension of its own. It was also a time when the relationship between Ghana and Togo, its eastern neighbour, was not cordial. Furthermore, it was a time when the country's economy was in a bad shape: the Economic Recovery Programme (ERP) and the Structural Adjustment Programme (SAP) had turned many people onto the streets as unemployed persons.

At civil society level, neither the relationship between the Togolese and Ghanaians nor that of the Liberians and Ghanaians could be described as cordial. The Togolese who sought asylum in Ghana were Ewe-speaking people and non-Ewe Ghanaians were suspicious of them, apparently because Ghana's ruling party was Ewe-biased (in spite of everything). Indeed, the Togolese opposition leader in exile in Ghana was Ewe and enjoyed all the benefits of a Ghanaian citizen as a result of his Ewe background and his opposition to the President of Togo who came from the northern part of Togo. The Liberians on their part could not enjoy the unqualified friendship of Ghanaians because in the wake of the civil war, some Ghanaians had been killed, maimed, or raped, and others had lost their property. Further, some of the Liberian refugees were said to have been guilty of these atrocities (Dick and Boer, 2001).

Sojourning in Ghana as refugees then, neither the Liberians nor the Togolese were very welcome guests. Furthermore, it was a time when many were living without humanitarian assistance (Dick, 2002b). It was against this background that the department in which I work, the Department of Sociology at the University of Cape Coast, decided to conduct a survey of the refugee camps in which they were kept (see also McCarthy, 1998).

Refugees as ethnic groups

For the purpose of this chapter, I shall refer to the refugees in the study as ethnic groups, specifically as secondary ethnic groups following the classification provided by E.K. Francis (1976). According to Francis, ethnics can be classified as primary or secondary ethnic groups. Primary ethnic groups are *viable corporate units*, which, after their transfer from the parent to the host society, tend to continue to function in the host society as closed sub-societies able to satisfy the basic needs of their members. In contrast, secondary ethnic groups are *subgroups of a parent society with diverse backgrounds*, who, having migrated to a host society in sufficient numbers and having suffered deprivations because of differential treatment in the host society, tend to form and maintain themselves as separate ethnic groups to compensate for these deprivations. The idea of nationalism among members of such groups tends to increase their awareness of identity and sense of solidarity and thus increases the likelihood of their secondary ethnic-group formation. To this end, separate institutions are created and upheld that exercise partial control over the group members. In sociological terms, secondary ethnic groups tend to be considered and treated as minority groups, but they need not always be so treated (Francis, 1976: 396–8). The process of integration of refugees into a host nation is, invariably, problematic (Jablasone, 2001).

The fact that the Liberians found themselves as a guest community in a camp situated in a Ghanaian community, in the first instance, made them see themselves as a minority group even though among themselves they recognized the different ethnic groups they belonged to way back home. In turn, they also were seen as such by their host community. Our survey identified eighteen ethnic groups among the Liberian refugees: the Kru,

Lorma, Gio, Bassa, Gissi, Belleh, Sarpo, Gola, Krahn, Manor, Congo, Gbandi, Kissi, Grebo, Vai, Day, Mende and Americo-Liberians (see also Dick, 2002a).

The Togolese refugees were more or less one homogenous group who described themselves as Ewes and were so recognized by their host community who were themselves also Ewe. Their close affinity to the host community, notwithstanding, the Togolese refugees could not be said to be welcome guests as their presence in Ghana at a difficult time meant competition for food, medical services, jobs, housing, and the environment (Kwadzo, 1993). In both cases, the presence of the Liberian and the Togolese refugees triggered off the conventional problem of inter-ethnic hostility between the host citizens and the guests.

Legally speaking, however, the Liberian and Togolese hosts come under the status of refugees as defined by Article 1 of the 1951 Geneva Refugee Convention. The Convention defines a refugee as:

A person who is outside his/her country of nationality or habitual residence; has a well-founded fear of persecution because of his/her race, religion, nationality, membership in a particular social group or political opinion; and is unable or unwilling to avail himself/herself of the protection of that country or return there, for fear of persecution (UNHCR, 2001).

Host governments are primarily responsible for protecting the refugees. Since Ghana is a party to the Convention, the government was obliged to carry out the provisions of the Convention even if it sympathized with the predicament of its own citizens. In this drama of the Liberian and Togolese refugees versus Ghanaian citizens, the government of Ghana can be described as an obliged host, while the citizens were the unwilling hosts and the refugees the unwanted but tolerated guests. This position of the refugees became even more pronounced and precarious as Ghanaians experienced rising waves of armed robberies, most of which were said to have been committed either by Liberians or by combined teams of Liberians and Ghanaians. Again, the refugees became the target of hostility from Ghanaian politicians in particular, because they were reported to have been used by the ruling party to rig votes during the 1992 multi-party elections.

Thus with the exception of the government, other stakeholders – workers, the unemployed, politicians, and families – did not take kindly to the refugees. Although there was no record of open physical violence against any of the refugees, the spate of verbal attacks was enough to warn them about the feelings of their civil and political hosts. What protected them against physical attack were the camps. Therefore, it was natural that the refugees felt safe in their camps and suspicious of visits by non-officials from the Ghanaian community. This position logically affected the survey, whose objective was to study the social and economic implications of the refugees in Ghana.

Accessing the refugees

Gaining physical access to the refugee camps was not much of a problem. A letter addressed to the Minister of Labour and Social Welfare on 16 February 1994 requesting permission to conduct a survey into the Social and Economic Implications of Refugeeism in Ghana opened the gate to the two camps for our research team. Gaining social access to the refugees was another matter. Our aim was to conduct the interviews by ourselves with the help of student assistants, but this was not possible because the refugees in neither camp could be convinced by the official attendants to grant us interviews face-to-face. It was even more difficult when we informed the camp attendants that we were going to take photographs of the camps and their inmates. In the end we had to abandon the idea of conducting the interviews ourselves and agreed to train some of the refugees to conduct them. The idea of taking pictures was also dropped. In this instance, flexibility in research plans was both ethical and methodologically prudent.

Allaying the fears of the respondents

The decision to use some of the refugees to administer the interviews under the supervision of the researchers turned out to be a blessing in disguise. In both camps, we came across refugees who were university students from their countries. Some of them were planning to seek admission to the universities in their host country. For them, it was welcome news to be involved in a social science research that targeted their fellow refugees in the camps. The two camps were the Buduburam camp on the western side of Ghana for the Liberians and the Klikor camp on the eastern side for the Togolese. Whereas the Liberian camp had a good mix of occupations and professionals, ranging from traders through to teachers, surveyors, business people, and public administrators, the Togolese camp was comprised mainly of traders, mechanics, farmers, and teachers. In addition, the Liberians were more educated than the Togolese. The average level of education for the Togolese was elementary school; in contrast, the majority of the Liberians had been through secondary school or higher education. The interviews among the Liberians therefore were conducted in most cases in English. There were a few cases where translations were made in the ethnic languages of the respondents. In contrast, interviews among the Togolese were conducted mostly in Ewe, with occasional translations in French.

These scenarios not only made interviewing easy, they also gave the refugees self-confidence and assured them of the protection they badly needed against possible identification. The data collection instrument also assured them of absolute anonymity and the interviewers were given strict instructions not to ask the names of the respondents or to say anything that would threaten the security of the respondents. With this reassurance, the respondents accepted the survey as their own and for their own good.

"Fears" of the refugees

The methodological approach dictated by the peculiarity of the refugee camps and the reaction of the refugees helped to dispel the fears of the refugees. And these fears were real! Among the Togolese there were two categories of people who feared repatriation. The first were traders and unemployed people who had taken advantage of the political situation to join the camp in the hope that they would be employed in the wake of Ghana's electoral process. These were, properly speaking, economic refugees. The second were criminals who had taken refuge in the camp in order to escape lawful arrest by their state security agents. Neither category of "asylum seeker" qualified as refugees as spelt out by the Geneva Convention referred to above.

In the Liberian Camp, there were three groups of people who were equally afraid of repatriation. These were those who had escaped lawful arrest as criminals; those who were wanted because of war atrocities committed by them as rebel soldiers; and those who had come to Ghana as economic refugees.

Reliability and validity of the responses

These fears could have marred the reliability and validity of the information we sought in our survey, but the fact that we used their fellow refugees as interviewers helped to reduce the error margin due to false answers. The instrument also had cross-checks to help validate responses. Questions such as: "Occupation/profession in your home country?"; "What conditions in your home country forced you to come and live in Ghana?"; "What changes would you like to take place in your country in order for you to decide to return home?"; and "Is there anything about life in Ghana which would make you decide not to return home even if the changes you desire take place there?", were built into the interview schedule. The purpose of these questions was to help make sense about the intentions of the respondents with regard to their decision to seek refuge in Ghana, their economic activities in Ghana and their future plans.

At this stage, it must be pointed out that the results from the survey cannot be said to be absolutely reliable. There were some instances where, for example, respondents gave their occupation as traders while at home, but claimed that they did not do "any work at the camp to earn money" and yet further down the interview, such respondents agreed that they "sell bread at the camp" in reaction to the question "explain how you get money for your personal expenses" (see also Kwadzo, 1994).

To test for validity of the responses, our team planned to back the one-on-one interviews with focus group discussions (FGDs). However, this was not possible due to lack of funds from the university that funded the survey. In any case, the plan for FGDs was abandoned because of our inability to have direct contact with the refugees.

Pooling the experiences together

The objective of the study was to examine the impact that the presence of refugees in Ghana could have on their host community, itself facing the adverse effects of ERP and SAP. The study was conducted almost five years after the arrival of the first refugees in Ghana. Even though the refugees were not directly competing in the employment market of the country, the fear that their hosts would construe their presence as a threat to their economic welfare was not unfounded. As has already been noted, this situation made the refugees not particularly welcome guests. The refugees consequently developed a defence mechanism – namely, an unwillingness to interact directly with non-official members of the Ghanaian community. This was the wall the research team encountered. The team could have ignored this defence wall by using the official channel to deal with the refugees directly. This would have been a professional blunder, and the price would have been too high for the survey for it would have meant the neglect of the ethics of social science research, which demands respect for human rights and the integrity of the subjects of research. Besides, it would have encouraged more incorrect responses from the participants.

The decision to use the refugees themselves as interviewers – as intermediaries – paid off. The price we paid was the need to find money to train them as interviewers. The price would have been higher if we had not met social science students in the camps. Again some, if not most, of the Togolese refugees and some of the Liberian refugees faced the threat of possible repatriation for either being economic refugees in Ghana or escaping lawful arrest for their criminal activities or war atrocities in their parent countries. For that matter, they had to be cautious about whom they talked to on the subject of their background. Although our instruments assured them of absolute anonymity, questions concerning their "ethnic background", "occupation in the home country", "conditions that forced the respondent to leave and come to Ghana" and the "number of times respondents had been able to visit their home country since he/she came to Ghana" could give leads to the types of refugees we had at the camps and therefore could raise the suspicion of the respondents.

Once again, the fact that the research team did not have direct contact with the refugees may have been a blessing in disguise. Technically, however, the cost of this was high, because we did not have the benefit of probing the responses and observing the respondents face-to-face in order to check whether or not they were telling the truth.

Some recommendations

With hindsight, we can perhaps recommend that in future, researchers who find themselves in a similar or even more complex situation such as we did should begin the fieldwork with a durbar or a forum comprising United Nations High Commissioner for Refugees representatives, host government officials, and spokespersons of the refugees in order to sensitize the latter to the objectives of the study and assure them of the protection of their human rights and identity in accordance with the spirit of the Geneva Convention on Refugees and the ethics of social science research. There are always new human rights challenges facing a government that emerges from destruction (Amnesty International, 2002; Human Rights Watch, 1997). Although the ethics of social science are not written in the form of a convention they are still morally binding on social science researchers.

The experience gained from the refugee study has prompted me to call on researchers of inter-ethnic relations and conflict situations throughout the world to establish a Convention on Conflict Studies just as we have the Geneva Convention on Refugees to guide researchers involved in conflict studies. The Convention should, among other things, cover issues such as professionalism, confidentiality, and respect for respondents, as well as the protection for researchers and participators who are the subjects of the studies.

These issues have not been addressed with the seriousness that they deserve in conventional textbooks on social research. Indeed, conventional social research methodology textbooks assume that fieldwork always takes place in conflict-free social contexts. The time has come to pay critical attention to the principles and ethics of social research methodology in current social contexts and in situations that are ridden with violent conflicts which thus call for new methodological approaches.

REFERENCES

Amnesty International/International Secretariat (2002) *Liberia: civilians face human rights abuses at home and across borders*, London: Amnesty International, p. 15.

Dick, Shelley and Boer, Wiebe (2001) "The spirits are angry: Liberia's secret cults in the service of civil war", *Books and Culture* 7(1): 26–27.

Dick, Shelley (2002a) *Responding to protracted refugee situation: A case study of Liberian refugees in Ghana*, Geneva: UNHCR Evaluation and Policy Analysis Unit (EPAU), p. 47. Online: http://www.unhcr.ch/cgibin/texis/vtx/home/opendoc.pdf?tbl=RESEARCH&id=3d40059b4&page=research.

—— (2002b) *Liberians in Ghana: Living Without Humanitarian Assistance*, UNHCR Working Paper No 57, Geneva, p. 74. Available online at: www.unhcr.ch/cgi-bin/texis/vtz/home.

Francis, Emerich K. (1976) *Inter-ethnic Relations: An Essay in Sociological Theory*, New York, Oxford and Amsterdam: Elsevier.

Human Rights Watch/Africa Report (1997) *Liberia: Emerging from the Destruction: Human Rights Challenges Facing the New Liberian Government*, New York/London: Human Rights Watch, p. 35.

Jablasone, J. (2001) *The Process of Integration of Refugees into a Host Nation: A Case Study of Liberian Refugees in Ghana*, Dissertation for a BA degree submitted to the Department of Social Sciences, University of Science and Technology, Kumasi.

Kwadzo, George T.-M. (1993) *Assessment of prospects for food self sufficiency by Togolese refugees in the Volta region*, prepared for WFP/UNHCR missions in Ghana, Legon, p. 62.

Kwadzo, George T.-M. and Amegashie, D.P.K. (1994) *Self-reliance of Togolese Refugee Households in Ghana*, prepared for WFP/UNHCR missions in Ghana, Legon, p. 138.

McCarthy, J. (1998) *The Management of Refugees Reception Centres in Ghana*, dissertation for BA degree submitted to Department of Development Planning, University of Science and Technology, Kumasi.

United Nations High Commissioner for Refugees (UNHCR) (2001) *Refugees – 50th Anniversary, The Wall Behind which Refugees can Shelter, the 1951 Geneva Convention*, Online: http://www.unhcr.ch/cgi-bin/texis/vtx/home/opendoc.pdf?id=3b5e90ea0&tbl=MEDIA.

5

Applying social work practice to the study of ethnic militias: The Oduduwa People's Congress in Nigeria

Isaac Olawale Albert

This chapter focuses on how the social work practice method can be used to study a militia movement. Social workers are, first and foremost, committed to people, their well-being, and to the enhancement of quality of life. In other words, the goal of social work is to help people in "difficult circumstances" overcome their social problems. A problem cannot be solved, however, unless properly understood. Social workers have diverse methods for understanding the people they work with and they also have methodologies for understanding the working environment. What I seek to do in this chapter is to demonstrate how such social work practice can serve as a field method for a researcher trying to gain deeper insight into the inner world of a militia movement. Projects carried out with members of the Oduduwa People's Congress (OPC) in Nigeria are used as a case study.

What constitutes an ethnic militia movement? We must start by defining what constitutes ethnicity. Cohen (1985: 119) defined ethnicity as "a mode of action and of representation: it refers to a decision people make to depict themselves or others symbolically as the bearers of a certain cultural identity". Where people have reasons to identify themselves as belonging to an ethnic group they are equally obligated to work towards defending that identity against other identities. It is the desire of members of any ethnic group to see it flourish and develop – sometimes at the expense of the people from other identity groups. It is within this context that ethnicity leads potentially to social tensions. Ethnic militias develop in a society where members of a particular ethnic group feel per-petually oppressed by a "ruling ethnic category".

Militias seek to achieve their set objectives through the use of physical violence. They rationalize their violent dispositions in terms of the phys-ical, psychological or structural violence that they perceive themselves and their jurisdiction to be subjected to by the group against which they now fight. To make the "battle-line" clear, they define their society in "us" and "them" terms: that is "we" (a group of "righteous" or "oppressed" people) against "they" (the "unrighteous" or "oppressors"). Militia groups do not necessarily see what they do as being morally right but rather expedient. All militias kill. They kill because of the perception that, if they do not, they themselves stand the risk of being eliminated by a rival group.

Two major types of militias exist around the world: those that use vio-lence to attain criminal goals and those that use violence to realize polit-ical objectives. The difference between the two is sometimes difficult to delineate because both the "criminal" and "political" militia operate out-side the law and, as far as the states in which they operate are concerned, they both are engaged in criminal activities. The campus cults in Nigerian universities are a textbook example of criminal militias. In several Latin American countries, there are militia groups that are organized around drugs trade. They fight against the government in defence of their "rights" to deal in narcotic drugs. My interest in this chapter is not on this kind of militia, however; the focus here is on political militia organ-izations. Three major types can be identified. The first is the ethnic type – namely, those that take up arms to defend the narrow interests of the ethnic jurisdiction they represent in a plural society. The second consists of those that focus on the narrow religious interests of the group they represent in a multi-religious state. The third consists of people from diverse ethnic and religious backgrounds who decide to come together with a view to defending an over-arching political interest. This third type of militia is usually organized around the question of democratic rights and popular participation. Our focus here is on the first group – those that pursue ethnic interests.

Problems associated with studying militia groups

From 29–31 October 2001, the *Institut Français de Recherche en Afrique* (IFRA-Ibadan), an agency of the French Ministry of Cooperation, hosted an International Conference on "Security, Segregation and Social Networks in West Africa, nineteenth and twentieth centuries" at the

University of Ibadan, Nigeria. The focus of the conference was on assessing the level of insecurity in West Africa and the contribution of social networks to the problem. This timely and well-attended conference drew participants from different parts of Africa and Europe. The international organizations represented included the Safer City Programme of the United Nations Centre for Human Settlement (Habitat), Nairobi.

I was a member of the three-man organizing committee for the conference. In our call for papers, we particularly asked prospective participants to take a critical look at the proliferation of militia movements (religious and ethnic) in West Africa. We received well over 50 abstracts, 13 of them focused on ethnic militias in Nigeria. We were not surprised about this given how the violent activities of such militia groups are threatening the nascent democracy in the country. However, while some had substance, it was clear that many Nigerians know too little about the militia groups tearing their society apart. This is rather unfortunate. Most of the papers were based on questionable hearsay and media reports, rather than field-based data. The limited information at the disposal of the authors was poorly analysed and not related to the existing knowledge, whether on ethnicity, or "vigilante politics", or "community policing" (Rosenbaum and Sederberg, 1976). Nigerian and European scholars at the conference had looked forward to a thorough discussion of the ethnic militia problems in Nigeria. In his report on the conference, the Director of IFRA singled out the issue of militia movements for "further investigation" (Fourchard, 2001).

Why was the subject matter of militia movements so poorly treated by the speakers at the IFRA conference? In my view, there is one simple answer: the authors wrote on the militant groups – most especially on OPC and Bakassi boys (BB) without actually moving close to them. As the Yoruba say "Oro okere bi kole kan, a din kan" (any second-hand information stands the risk of being either exaggerated or understated). There are two possible explanations: the IFRA presenters either lacked the financial resources for doing fieldwork among the militias or they were afraid of moving too close to the groups. The daredevil imagery of the OPC and BB in the Nigerian media is enough reason for nonprofessionals in security studies to maintain a safe distance from the groups. The public image of the "boys", which has been significantly drummed up by the federal government of Nigeria and its coercive agencies – most especially the police – is that of a group that strikes without warning and kills without any human considerations. The groups also have an image of being a law unto themselves. They define crimes, sometimes unconventionally, and award "appropriate punishments" for them.

The existing literature shows that there is nothing unique about this Nigerian situation. In many other parts of the world, militia groups operate outside the law and scholars who study them consider themselves to be doing "dangerous fieldwork". It is important to try to shed light on why scholars often run away from doing "dangerous fieldwork". The reasons include the physical, environmental, and biological hazards that could confront the researcher. A researcher studying a violent group could be hurt or even killed by the group or its adversaries and there are instances going back to the early years of the twentieth century when anthropologists were killed by the people they were studying. Rubin and Rubin (1995: 7) talk of the possibility of "getting to an appointment and finding the interviewee sitting in the middle of the room with a shotgun in his lap". The rate of violence in the world is increasing, suggesting that more researchers could still be killed in violent societies. This concern is justified readily by the number of journalists that are killed in situations of armed conflict and war around the world. There is no major armed conflict or war around the world that does not have its own toll of dead journalists. Researchers who work in such dangerous settings also stand the risk of getting killed. But unlike journalists, the death of academic researchers operating in a war zone will go unsung. There are implications from all these problems, as they shape research agendas by deterring researchers from investigating specific topics or working in particular regions. Consequently, research strategies adopted to manage such potential hazards, both for researchers themselves and for those they study, have practical implications in the ethics and politics of field situations.

A disinclination to face physical risks is not the only reason why people shy away from doing dangerous research. Boldness of heart is not all that researchers need. They have to contend with problem of access – both to the setting and "extracting useful answers" from the researched. Dangerous settings hardly provide the room for researchers to be ordinary in the efforts to establish the needed credibility before the informant. Some researchers might find this challenge too gargantuan to contend with. The researcher could do three possible things in addressing this problem. The first is to identify with whatever the group represents. In this case, the researcher claims to be an "insider" and is treated as such by the group if his or her explanations are accepted as plausible. The second alternative is to claim to be an outsider but assure individuals in the group that the information provided will be treated with utmost confidentiality. The third is to engage an insider to act as a "research assistant" in the project and through the latter gain access to some privileged information about the group. Each of these approaches has its merits and demerits.

As an insider, the general assumption is that the researcher already knows about the group to be studied. The fieldwork here will be very interesting if one is dealing with an esoteric subject. An insider studying deviant behaviour such as criminal and political violence might not have all the necessary information at his fingertips, as one would naturally expect. Secrecy is the hallmark of people operating in dangerous terrains. Asking "basic questions" about a violent movement could readily ignite some doubt and queries about the true identity of the "insider". Questions might include: "Hasn't he become a sell-out?", "What is she going to do with so much esoteric information about us?", "Can we really trust his intentions?". The other point that must be noted is that a "committed insider" will not want to betray his or her movement by sharing with "outsiders" internal secrets of the group. In other words, the insider's perspective might not be as easily obtainable as we might assume.

The "outsider" who promises to treat the information given to him confidentially risks being treated with greater suspicion. Likely questions include: "Why is she asking questions about us?", "Who sent him?", "What interests does she represent?" Members of militia movements might be careless with many things, but not confidential information about themselves. The ordinary members sometimes are not trusted with confidential information, not to mention those that describe themselves as "outsiders". We can illustrate this with the example of Afghanistan. In the dimly lit hour-long video film implicating Osama Bin Laden in the 11 September 2001 attacks on the World Trade Centre and the Pentagon, the prime suspect noted that none of the suicide bombers sent on the mission had any information about the assignments they were to carry out until a few minutes into their boarding the ill-fated aeroplanes. As Bin Laden noted in the tape:

The brothers who conducted the operation, all they knew was that they have a martyrdom operation, and we asked each of them to go to America but they didn't know anything about the operation, *not even one letter*. But they were trained and we did not reveal the operation to them until they were there and just before they boarded the planes ... Those who were trained to fly didn't know the others. One group of people did not know the other group (*Newsweek*, 24 December 2001, pp. 14–15; my italics).

The video film, believed to have been filmed on 9 November 2001, was obtained in early December 2001 from a house in Jahalabad, Afghanistan. It showed Bin Laden addressing his confidants in the al-Qaeda and Taliban movements. The video must have been produced for "internal consumption" and not what it was later used for (an exhibit against Bin Laden). Bin Laden could not have talked to a researcher (academic or media journalist) so freely. Indeed, leaders of violent movements cannot confide in their followers; operational information is protected. No leader of a militant group lets out confidential information about operational tactics. A researcher working with such a group from outside might therefore end up getting no more than 10 per cent of what needs to be known, if given any audience at all.

Researching into a violent society is a dangerous and painstaking task, which many modern-day researchers are not willing to undertake. This explains why we have too few scholars in the world today who can be said to be experts in studying violent societies. To be said to be an expert suggests that a person has gained mastery over a system as a result of doing it over and over again. One cannot become an expert when not willing to take even the first step.

The Oduduwa People's Congress as an ethnic militia

The OPC is one of the most popular militia movements in Nigeria; others include the Bakassi and Egbesu movements. The emergence of the OPC is connected closely with the popular 12 June crisis in Nigeria. On 12 June 1993, a presidential election, said by both foreign and Nigerian assessors to have been the fairest and freest in the history of Nigeria, was annulled by the administration of General Ibrahim Badamosi Babangida. All the official excuses given by the Nigerian military for the annulment were considered popularly to be escapist and far-fetched. The annulment therefore was not accepted by the majority of Nigerians except by those Rotimi and Ihonvbere (1994: 674) rightly dismissed as "intellectual rationalizers, hangers-on, opportunists and contractors". The annulment was subject to all forms of interpretation. The candidate for the annulled election, Chief M.K.O. Abiola, was a Yoruba man and it was the first time that a Yoruba person had ever won a presidential election in Nigeria. The annulment therefore could not but be given an ethnic interpretation. Southern Nigerians generally saw it as evidence of the reluctance of the northerners (who had been ruling Nigeria since the 1960 independence) to surrender political power to the other ethnic groups in Nigeria. The Yoruba particularly interpreted the development as clear evidence that northern Nigerians, the interests of which Babangida was believed to have represented, did not want a Yoruba person to rule Nigeria.

The political crisis generated by the annulment forced President Babangida to vacate the seat of power on 26 August 1993. Without an enabling decree, he handed over power to an Interim National Government (ING) headed by Chief Ernest Shonekan, a fellow Egba man and Yoruba with Chief M.K.O. Abiola. The game plan was to use this to appease the Yoruba people or to break the rank and file of the 12 June agitators. It did not work. The Yoruba simply tagged Chief Shonekan a political opportunist and traitor, and the government he headed was seen as a fraud and an extension of the Babangida's military and northern Nigerian administration. The people insisted that the 12 June results should be announced and Abiola sworn into office. The Governors of Oyo, Ogun, Osun and Ondo states (Yoruba states) simply refused to recognize Shonekan as their head of state. The governors and other prominent Yoruba sons and daughters also advised all Yoruba people in the ING to resign their appointments (*Tell*, 12 September 1993, pp. 16–17). Several court cases were instituted to challenge the legality or otherwise of the ING. On 10 November 1993, the ING was declared unconstitutional, illegal, and therefore a nullity in a ruling at the Lagos High Court presided over by Justice J. Akinsanya. General Sani Abacha, who was the then Minister for Defence used this as an excuse to seize power from Shonekan on 17 November 1993. The north was now fully back to power. This new development and the punitive policy pursued against the Yoruba people by the administration of General Abacha between 1993 and 1998 heightened the political tension in south-western Nigeria (see Amuwo et al., 2001). It was within this framework that the OPC was born.

The OPC describes itself, first and foremost, as "Egbe ajija gbara" (freedom fighters). The OPC did not start as a violent organization; it was forced by the repressive policies of the Abacha regime (through the police) to become violent. When established in 1994 by a group led by Dr. Frederick Faseun, the main goal of the OPC was to serve as an agency through which the Yoruba people could speak with one voice on issues pertaining to their corporate interests in the Nigerian state. The organization is also supposed to be a forum for debating and protecting the Yoruba interests. The number one objective of the group was to work towards the creation of an "Oduduwa state" out of the present Nigerian society if political solutions to the Nigerian problems proved abortive. At the initial stage, the organization adopted a non-violent strategy.

The OPC became a violent organization in 1996 for a number of reasons. Right from its inception, the OPC was perceived by the Abacha regime as a secessionist organization. The police therefore disrupted all its meetings. In the process, several OPC members were killed, maimed, or subjected to long periods of detention without trial. The non-violent disposition of Dr. Faseun prevented the OPC from taking any major reprisal action against the police. The situation started to change in 1996 when Faseun was arrested by the officials of the Abacha regime on account of being engaged in "subversive activities". This made members of the group start to rethink their strategies. By the time Faseun came out of detention, his "tread-softly" policy was no longer acceptable to the boys he was leading. The boys wanted full military training rather than the "paper tiger" that Faseun wanted OPC to be. The commitment of Faseun to the cause of the Yoruba soon began to be doubted by members of the group. The problem of Faseun became compounded in 1999 during the political transition programme that saw Obasanjo becoming the Nigerian Head of State. Faseun wanted OPC members to be part of the political transition; a faction of the group insisted that OPC must stay outside partisan politics and focus more on how to "liberate" the Yoruba people. Faseun was soon accused of corruption. A member of the OPC claimed to have seen him collecting money from Chief Obasanjo to advance Obasanjo's political interests. OPC thus broke into two factions: the Gani Adam's faction favoured a violent solution to the Nigerian problems and the Faseun faction remained more compromising in addressing the Yoruba problems.

The Gani Adam's faction of the OPC sees itself as a true ethnic militia. The group differentiates itself from the other faction by addressing itself as "OPC Militant". The group believes in the healing power of political violence and is not euphemistic about attaining its objectives through the use of violence. The world of the group is captured indirectly by Nechayev (cited by Rapoport, 1971: 79) when he notes that:

The revolutionary is a dedicated man. He has no personal inclinations, no business affairs, no emotions, no attachments, no property, and no name. Everything in him is subordinated towards a single exclusive attachment, a single thought, and a single passion – the revolution ... he has torn himself away from the bonds which tie him to the social order and to the cultivated world, with all its laws, moralities, and customs ... The revolutionary despises public opinion ... morality is everything which contributes to the triumph of the revolution. Immoral and criminal is everything that stands in his way ... Night and day he must have but one thought, one aim – merciless destruction ... he must be ready to destroy himself and destroy with his own hands everyone who stands in his way.

During one of the projects reported in this chapter, I posed the question to the OPC members: "Why are you fighting?" They claimed to be fighting because Nigeria is a failed project led by criminally minded blind men. The Yoruba have divine reasons not to be at their present low level of development, therefore "Ile Ya"! ("the homeward journey is now"). The OPC blames all the development problems faced by Nigeria – political instability, economic stagnation, official and unofficial criminality – on the Hausa-Fulani. The group does not believe that the Hausa-Fulani "problem" can be solved non-violently. It is therefore often quick to blame the problems faced by the Yoruba people in Nigeria on past leaders of the group "who preached peace for so many generations and left us nowhere". Members of the organization therefore look forward to a period when the Yoruba "nation" would finally "exit" from the unjust Nigerian federation.

"Exit" as used above is a recent euphemism for secession. Following Azarya (1988), Azarya and Chazan (1987), Bayart (1999), Haynes (1997), and others, the term was defined by Osaghae (1999: 83) as "disengagement or retreat from the state by disaffected segments of the citizenry into alternative and parallel social, cultural, economic and political systems which are constructed in civil society and which compete with those of the state". A major characteristic of an exiting entity is that it tries to submerge the state with its spectacular claims and mobilizations (Bayart, 1999) and as du Toit (1995: 31) observed, exit is a survival strategy of the weak and marginalized in "a domineering yet ineffective state". Osaghae tried to enrich our understanding of this concept by differentiating between what he referred to as "exit from the polity" which bypasses organized civil order and "exit from the state" which is more explicitly political. Trying to differentiate between the two, Osaghae (1999) further notes that both forms of exit renounce the state's responsibility for welfare and security thereby diminishing the citizen's loyalty and prompting ethnic, religious, or deviant anti-system identities.

The expectation of exiting from the Nigerian state is a refrain at every OPC meeting. It is deeply reflected in the "National Anthem" of the group that is sung before the start and at the end of every OPC meeting:

Ile ya
Ile ya O, Omo Oduduwa Ile ya
Ti a koba mo'bi ta'nre
Oye ka pada si'le
Ka jawo lapon ti koyo
Ka lo gbo'mi'la kana
Ile ya
Ile ya O, Omo Oduduwa Ile ya

Homeward journey
Sons of Oduduwa, The time for the homeward journey is now!
If we don't know where we [the Yoruba in Nigeria] are being taken to
Why don't we beat a retreat now?
We should push aside the "apon" soup that fails to live up to expectation
And start preparing okro as an alternative
Homeward journey
Sons of Oduduwa, This is the time for the homeward journey.

Since 1996 when it became an ethnic militia, the OPC had been implicated in various types of political violence in south-western parts of Nigeria. The terrain of these violent ethnic clashes included Ogun, Lagos, Oyo, Osun, Kwara, and Ondo states. Most of these violent ethnic conflicts in which they were involved were between the Hausa-Fulani people and the Yoruba. The OPC, in each of the incidents, fought on the side of the Yoruba people. Most of the OPC insurgencies are against the Hausa-Fulani settlers in Yorubaland. The OPC are also involved in the ethnic politics of Ilorin, a town between northern and southern Nigeria. The goal of the OPC is to reverse the past trend that enabled the Fulani to lord it over (through the traditional political institutions) the Yoruba, who constitute the larger population in the settlement. The OPC seeks to install a Yoruba king (Oba) in Ilorin to serve as a rival to the present Emir of the town. As far as the OPC are concerned, Ilorin is a Yoruba town and should not be ruled by a Fulani Emir, who represents the Hausa-Fulani interests. The OPC saga led to a drastic deterioration of Yoruba–Hausa-Fulani relations in Nigeria. The two are now locked in a conflict of a national magnitude. This problem, directly and indirectly, threatens the success of the nascent democracy in Nigeria. To ease tension in the land, the Obasanjo administration had to proscribe the OPC in 2000. The organization however is still waxing strong, both underground and in the open. Nigerians popularly see the OPC as "the IRA of the Yoruba nation"; that is, a terrorist organization.

The OPC also engage in "crime control vigilantism" (Rosenbaum and Sederberg, 1976). Believing that the Nigerian police are too inefficient to ensure the protection of law and order in Yorubaland, the OPC members have constituted themselves into an alternative police force. They arrest criminals in the society and mete out "appropriate punishments". The most common of these is the lynching (beating and sometimes nailing to a cross) of thieves, armed robbers, and "419ers" (people engaged in scams). In the process of such extra-judicial crime control and prevention measures, the OPC is known to have killed many innocent people, including policemen. Some Yoruba people therefore, are opposed to the violent disposition of the group. The most recent in the series of accusations against the OPC is that some Yoruba leaders use members of the organization to settle personal scores with their enemies.

Ethnic reality and social work practice

Published works on social work practice with militant movements are difficult to come across. Social workers are more at home with working on family violence – child abuse, elder abuse, wife abuse – (Dobash and Dobash, 1992; Kingston and Penhale, 1995; Langan and Day, 1992; Phillipson, 1992). This is understandable. Whereas family-related problems are usually within the private domain and can therefore be dealt with at individual levels, issues of political violence are usually within the public domain; they have to do with groups and often are very delicate to be delved into by social workers. State officials best handle them with responsibility for ensuring the maintenance of law and order; or they can be handled by non-governmental organizations (NGOs) promoting non-violent social change. Most of the NGOs however, adopt social work practice methodologies in working with the violent groups or parties. What are these approaches to social work practice to which NGOs sometimes resort?

The emphasis of social work practice is in a deepening understanding of human conditions, the causes of such conditions, and translating such understanding of how people function into principles for problem resolution. Like medical doctors, the work of social workers involves: diagnosis, prognosis, and treatment. "Diagnosis" involves finding out what the problem is, "prognosis" requires a critical investigation of where the problem is now and where it is likely to degenerate to later, and "treatment" is the application of the right kind of medication.

Social workers use four main approaches for coming to terms with the problems faced by the groups they seek to help: first, the psychosocial approach; second, the problem-solving approach; third, the social provision and structural approach; and fourth, the systems approach.

First, the *psychosocial approach* to social work practice emphasizes the importance of personal pathology in the aetiology of social problems. The main argument in the psychosocial approach to social work practice is that human conditions are shaped by the unique past histories of the specific group and the internal dynamic generated by those histories. The psychosocial approach posits that the family, the social group, and the community impact heavily on social functioning and so breakdown in social adjustment of individuals can translate into a community-wide problem. Psychosocial therapy can help people shape their destiny.

The second *problem-solving approach*, assumes that past experiences, present perception of one's situation and reaction to the problem, and also future aspirations combine to define the person with a problem. Today's reality is, however, the most important thing to take into consideration in evaluating the person and assessing what reform is necessary. The goal of this problem-solving approach is to provide interpersonal resources to deal with present problem-ridden situations (Devore and Schlesinger, 1981: 110).

The third *social provision and structural approach* emphasizes the role of structural inequity as a source of social tension. Individual problems are perceived as a function of social disorganization rather than as individual pathology. Social problems emerge in a context of social institutional sources of stress. Social workers must therefore understand individualized institutional membership (Siporin, 1975) and improve the relationships between people and their environments (Germain, 1979).

The three approaches mentioned above inform interventive procedures. The *systems approach*, which is the fourth, sees social problems in systemic terms: one part affects the other. The approach avoids the efforts made in the earlier three approaches at dichotomizing between person/environment, clinical practice/social action, and microsystem/ macrosystem; it argues rather that the strength of social work practice should lie in working with the interconnectedness between these elements (Pincus and Minahan, 1973). This approach calls the attention of social workers to five important social issues that could serve as sources of social tensions. They are, first, the absence of resources needed to achieve goals, solve problems, alleviate distress, accomplish life tasks, or realize aspirations and values (Devore and Schlesinger, 1981: 125); second, the absence of linkages between people and resource systems or between resource systems; third, problematic interaction between people within the same resource system; fourth, problematic interaction between resource systems; and fifth, problematic individual internal problem-solving or coping resources.

Social work practice and the Oduduwa People's Congress "fieldwork"

Issues that lead to disintegration in a society include problems of individual and group self-realization, self-actualization, and equality of opportunity. Social workers believe, very strongly, that a divided society can be "corrected". The first step is to make each member of such a society see him or herself as being intrinsically valuable, with the capacity to change and grow. People must grasp the need for personal and social responsibility and be willing to contribute to the enhancement of peace in the community. To this end, social workers invest much of their energies on the promotion of communal spirit in ethnically divided societies (Devore and Schlesinger, 1981).

A problem that is not known cannot be solved. In working on ethnically sensitive issues, social workers try to look at problems as defined by their clients. They allow their clients to identify the issues they consider to be important in the social conflict. This provides the social worker with the opportunity to gauge feelings about the problems at hand. This promotes warmth, empathy, and genuineness and as Devore and Schlesinger (1981: 175) note, "feelings, particularly those of a negative nature, must often be expressed before people can move forward to consider facts or suggestions for action". A social worker's perception of a problem could be misleading, most especially in seeking the best way to solve the problem. Conflict management practitioners are conscious of this wisdom. They allow conflict parties to present their problems, as they perceive them. It is not part of the responsibility of the professional conflict manager to obstruct effective communication or pass a judgement on who is right or wrong. Through joint problem-solving working sessions, largely involving the asking and answering of questions, each party to the conflict is made to see what aspects of his or her personality, and what issues, rules, or structures, have to be transformed in order to have peace. The decision on how to solve the problem can then be taken collectively.

In apprehending the nature of the problems faced by the OPC, reference was made to the four social work approaches dealt with above and the issues raised in the last paragraph. Particular attention was paid to ascertaining the link between an individual and a group's functioning and the social situation in which they find themselves. These gave us insight into the kind of disease we were out to treat and how it should be treated.

We found the systems approach most appealing for understanding the OPC, given that it has some elements of the other approaches. The approach was adopted in the project to gain insights into the problems of the ethnic militia and in designing our technical responses. The OPC perceive the problem of the Yoruba people in terms of a people who have been denied a very important resource – power – for too long. They are more disturbed by the fact that the Hausa-Fulani, who are so denying political power, are "not as intelligent, hardworking or politically articulate" as the Yoruba. They blame the political dominance of the Hausa-Fulani on the British colonial rule, greediness on the part of some Yoruba leaders, and the way elections are rigged in Nigeria. They blame almost all the problems in the Nigerian society on the Hausa-Fulani – political instability, poor leadership, corruption, youth unemployment, and so on. The OPC feels that the Yoruba will develop more rapidly if it could successfully opt out of the Nigerian state. The group believes at the same time that the Hausa-Fulani would not let either the Yoruba or Igbo secede from the country. The only way to do it therefore is to resort to political violence. Indirectly making reference to the 12 June crisis, the OPC members are quick to say "Violence is the only thing that the Hausa-Fulani cannot annul". The determination of the OPC to use force is explained partly by their belief that the Nigerian state is doomed in its present form:

If you fight you might be killed, if you don't you are sure of being killed by hunger and deprivation which our leaders have built into our political system; why not fight today, gain a victory and leave a future for the coming generation?

The researcher and social work practice

The privilege of using social work practice to study the OPC was "conferred" on me by the advantage I had, serving as a consultant to the United States Agency for International Development/Office of Transition Initiatives (USAID/OTI) from 2000 to 2001. I designed and actively participated in the implementation of several of the projects undertaken by the organization in Nigeria. This afforded me the opportunity of building my research agenda into some of the works. Wherever we went we worked with the local people, but I listened carefully for new concepts, themes, ideas, and stories that could help me to have a better understanding of the militant communities in which our works were done. As I listened with one ear as a social worker, I listened with the other as a researcher. I produced two books at the end of the OTI projects in Nigeria (Albert, 2001a, Albert, 2001b) though neither addressed the question of research methodology, but how "interventions" could be and were organized in Nigeria.

The two OPC projects focused on in this study took place at Oke-Ogun area of Oyo state and Akure, the capital of Ondo state. The fieldwork methods that we will be discussing in this chapter include how we gained access, how we made our qualitative observations, and how we did our qualitative interviews at group and individual levels. In organizing each of these activities, I relied on my past field experiences with projects funded in different parts of Nigeria and Africa by the Department for International Development (DFID), the Urban Management Programme (UMP) and the US Agency for International Development (USAID).

It is necessary to shed light on the circumstances leading to the Oke-Ogun and Akure interventions before going further to discuss our data collection methods during the projects. The Oke-Ogun project had to do with promoting peaceful co-existence between the Fulani pastoralists in Oke-Ogun area and the local Yoruba farmers, with whom the former were always locked in violent conflicts. The Akure project was aimed at training OPC members in non-violent conflict resolution and, by doing so, making them an asset rather than a liability to the on-going political transition in Nigeria. We need to shed more light on each of the projects.

The Fulani people of Nigeria live in northern parts of the country. During the dry season, when green grasses can no longer be found in the north, the pastoralists migrate on foot to the south with their livestock, crossing several farmlands. Unavoidably, some of the animals trespass into local farmlands. Violent conflict between local farmers and the Fulani pastoralists are a daily occurrence in different parts of Nigeria – most especially during the dry season. The Oke-Ogun area of Oyo state, consisting of eleven local government councils, constitutes the borderland between the north and south-western Nigeria. It is therefore the first part of south-western Nigeria (Yorubaland) that the pastoralists reach as they move towards the coastal city of Lagos. As the pastoralists in the Oke-Ogun move their livestock from one part of the area to the other, they usually clash with the local farmers.

The Fulani-farmer conflicts in the Oke-Ogun area started to have an ethnic garb between 1994 and 1998 when General Sani Abacha was Nigeria's Head of State. Before this period, some Fulani pastoralists who were not interested in engaging the local farmers in a bloody duel would offer to compensate farmers whose farms were destroyed by the migrating livestock herds. As soon as Abacha became the Nigerian president, the Fulani people were said to have stopped paying compensation. The attempts made by some of these farmers to force the pastoralists to pay compensation led to a series of bloody clashes. Any time such hostility broke out, the Hausa and Fulani people of Oke-Ogun would take their case to Alhaji Haruna Mai Yasin Katsina, who was himself a pastoralist before becoming the head of the Hausa community at Shasha Ibadan, (the Sarkin Sasa). Mai Yasin Katsina was very influential during the Abacha regime. He was believed to be one of the marabouts (spiritualists) consulted by the late Nigerian dictator. On account of the closeness between the two, Abacha was believed to have given one of his daughters to him for marriage. As we (Albert, Olaoba, and Adekola, 2001: 25) noted in an earlier study:

Haruna personified the regime of General Abacha in Ibadan and is remembered to have defied local authorities in Ibadan in all forms – threatening each time to drag his adversaries before the late Head of State. His Hausa subjects and loyalists, living around Bodija, Ojo and Sasa, are also believed to have committed different kinds of atrocities against the Yoruba people in Alhaji Katsina's name.

The popular opinion about the exploits of the Sarkin Sasa is partly reiterated in an editorial in the *Sunday Tribune* of 15 October 1995, addressed to the Governor of Oyo State, Colonel Ike Nwosu, by some Ibadan indigenes who simply described themselves as "sons of the soil" for security reasons:

The perpetual claim of Mai Yasin as the spiritual guardian and in-law of the Head of State – General Sani Abacha is in bad faith which frightens the people and threatens the peace of Nigeria especially Ibadan and its environs. Alhaji Haruna has constituted himself into a tin god by his utterances and his conduct has been rivalling the traditional position of the Olubadan of Ibadanland, we regard this as an affront to the Royal Stool of His Highness. The Shasha Quarters is a small community under a recognized traditional Baale of Ibadanland who is a traditional Chieftain of the Olubadanland. The Seriki Shasha is a subject under the traditional Baale of Shasha community and is at the same time a chieftain under Seriki Hausawa of Ibadanland. His [Mai Yasin's] personal arrogance is even manifested in his lifestyle for example. He also uses Pilot vehicles with in-built siren systems. What is more, he moves about Ibadan City and environs with lorry loads of armed Police escorts who have constituted themselves into terror and public nuisance. He doth bestride the whole of Ibadan City a Colossus.

There was not much anybody could do to curb how the Sarkin Sasa was conducting himself. He had the ears of the powers-that-be at Abuja and the Yoruba people of Oyo state saw his activities as a continuation of the Abacha's "punitive expedition" against the Yoruba people following the annulled 12 June election.

The Sarkin Sasa responded promptly to all "distress calls" made by his kinsmen at Oke-Ogun area. Policemen were sent to arrest the Yoruba people with whom the pastoralists had conflicts. Some of these Yoruba people are said to have died in detention. The fear of Sarkin Sasa made the tension in the area calm down. The Yoruba people who had their crops destroyed by livestock passing through their farms consoled themselves and interpreted the whole thing as the "work of God". This was the situation when Chief Obasanjo – a Yoruba man who was imprisoned by General Abacha – became the Nigerian Head of State on 29 May 1999. The Yoruba people of Oke-Ogun resolved to stop the incessant destruction of their farms by the Fulani pastoralists. Violence, once again, resumed at this part of Oyo State. The OPC came into the conflict on the side of the Yoruba farmers. The conflict escalated to higher heights with the Fulani suffering heavy losses on each occasion there was a clash. With time, the conflict became a national issue with the leaders of the Arewa Consultative Council (ACF) threatening to launch a reprisal attack on the Yoruba settlers in Northern Nigeria if the Oke-Ogun violence did not stop. It was at this point that USAID/OTI came into the matter to broker peace between the two warring parties.

The focus of the Oke-Ogun intervention was to promote non-violence between the Yoruba farmers and Fulani pastoralists in the Oke-Ogun area. The OPC were brought into the project because of the roles they played in the ethnic violence. Our goal here as researchers was to transform positively the perception of the OPC members on how to respond to conflict situations. The OPC members that attended the Iseyin meeting represented their other colleagues in the eleven local government council areas of Oke-Ogun. The workshops took place in May and June 2000 and lasted for three weeks during which the Yoruba farmers, Fulani pastoralists, and leaders of the OPC in the area were brought together to discuss their differences. At the end of the project, the three groups resolved to establish a peace-monitoring group, which is still in existence today.

Unlike the Oke-Ogun project that was a "local" affair, the Akure workshops were a national project. The workshops were meant for OPC members drawn from all parts of south-western Nigeria (consisting of six states of the Nigerian federation), and Kwar and Kogi states from the Middle Belt. The goal was to promote the culture of non-violence in the leadership of the movement. The Akure workshops lasted for three weeks in May 2001. The training programme was broken into three parts with each lasting for four days. The first workshop was for leaders of the OPC movement. The invitees consisted of both national and state leaders (chairmen, secretaries, and other principal officer holders). Dr. Frederick Faseun himself led the Faseun faction to the meeting. Evangelist Adesokan, then secretary of the faction, led the Gani Adams faction. (Gani Adams was still wanted by the police at this time.) The second batch of workshop participants consisted of the "Eshos". These are "war commanders", leaders of the "foot soldiers" during each of the violent encounters in which the OPC members were involved. Several of the "Eshos" are herbalists and believe very much in the efficacy of super-natural forces in political violence. The third workshop, which was the last, was meant for representatives of the first two groups. This last group was the one charged with the responsibility for working out the peace terms between the factions and seeing to the building of the culture of non-violence in the movement.

The data collection methods

The two projects presented above provided ample opportunities for data collection on the OPC movement. Opportunities for sourcing of academic data made themselves available at the conception, implementa-tion, monitoring, and evaluation stages of the work. Each of these stages produced its own unique kind of research data. One of the issues dealt with at the first stage was a group discussion on problems of access and risk management. The discussion on the "problem of access" focused on how to attain three types of credibility before the OPC members: per-sonal credibility of the coordinator; institutional credibility of the organ-izations represented by the coordinator; and procedural credibility of the intervention. If we could get over these three problems, the risk of the project would be minimized.

"Personal credibility" had to do with the moral space occupied by whoever was informing the OPC about the project. The major questions we expected the OPC to ask were, "Who are you?", "What are your antecedents?", and "Do you have the moral credentials for posing as a social worker before us?". The OPC members also would want to be assured that they were dealing with a trustworthy institution. The questions asked on "institutional credibility" therefore would have included "Which institution do you represent?", "What right has the organization to come into our camp this easily?", "Why is your organization sponsoring the project?", "What is the moral space occupied by your organization?" For procedural credibility, the questions we expected to be asked by the OPC included: "How are you going to achieve your set objectives?" "What are you offering that some other groups have not offered in the past?" "What are your expected outcomes?" and "Whose interest would such outcome serve?" If we answered these questions plausibly, the OPC boys would welcome our intervention. If we failed to answer the questions well, the boys might not cooperate with us. We carefully developed some working answers to the questions and asked our representatives to take these answers to the OPC.

Reaching the OPC in the Oke-Ogun project was not too difficult. We approached the chairmen of the local government councils in the Oke-Ogun area who had been making efforts to resolve the farmer–pastoralist conflicts before our intervention. Some OPC members had held meetings with some of these chairmen in the past. There were therefore no personal or institutional credibility problems to deal with. The chairmen simply dealt with the procedural credibility issue by telling the OPC boys that USAID/OTI has a globally recognized image of helping divided societies to work on their problems. Through these local government chairmen, the leaders of the OPC movement in the Oke-Ogun area agreed to attend our conflict resolution workshops, held in Iseyin. The OPC came to the workshops as a united front. A chairman of the Faseun faction led the delegation assisted by a secretary of the Adams' faction. All the decisions reached at the meeting had the blessing of the two factions.

The Akure meeting was planned more carefully. This was because it involved more risks than the Oke-Ogun situation. A brainstorming session on the project had to be organized. The discussion took place between the USAID/OTI programme manager in charge of the intervention, a leading human rights activist who was asked to coordinate the project, and myself as the project consultant. We carefully debated: "What should go into the intervention, why and how?", "How do we establish contacts with the OPC members?" and "How do we bring the two factions of the OPC without the two clashing?". This last question became necessary given the way the two factions clashed, leading to loss of lives and property, when the attempt was made by the Ooni of Ife (the titular head of the Yoruba race) to reconcile them. We also had some other problems to contend with such as what the reaction of the Nigerian security officials would be when the news eventually filtered to them that we had a working relationship with the OPC, an outlawed militia movement. The risks were many but we were determined to push ahead with the OPC project. Our strong belief was that the project would make a significant impact on the building of a culture of peace in Nigeria. In the course of this initial group discussion, we developed strategies for handling each of the security questions.

Gani Adams, a factional leader of the OPC, was still wanted by the police by the time we conducted the workshops. A prize was on his head; he was wanted dead or alive. There was also a presidential order at the time that anybody who paraded himself as an OPC member should not just be arrested but shot at sight. Getting the OPC members to attend the Akure meeting therefore required a high level of institutional credibility. The person appointed to coordinate the project was a great asset as he had the right kind of personal credibility for the job. This helped us in many other aspects. He was given the assignment on the account that he would play the role of an "insider" in the project very well. Though no longer an active member of the movement, the co-coordinator of the project (as a human rights activist) was part of the discussions leading to the formation of the OPC movement in 1994. He knows the leaders of the movement intimately; they too know him as a man who will not betray them. As the Yoruba say:

A ki bawo je
Ka bawo mu
Ka dale awo

It is unethical to eat with the other cult members
Drink with them
And turn round to betray your fellow cultists.

This was the wisdom that enabled us to merit the right kind of institutional credibility when our coordinator eventually approached the OPC members. Through him, we established contacts with the two factions of the movement and an agreement was reached on why, when, and where the conflict management-training workshop should be held.

The meaning of the OPC intervention would have been misinterpreted (most especially by the Nigerian government and the Hausa-Fulani population) if it was done in the name of any existing non-governmental organization in south-western Nigeria. The decision therefore was reached to carry out the project in the name of "Yoruba Solidarity Agenda". This gave the OPC boys, the coordinator of the project, and the rest of us (project facilitators) some "protection". The OPC members came to Akure as "Yoruba Youths" and we came to the meeting as "Youth Leadership Trainers". This, however, did not deter security men

– most especially officials of the State Security Service (SSS) – from showing up at the workshop when it started. They came to the meeting, in their words, not to disrupt it but to give us "security cover". The OPC boys and their leaders are well-known to Nigerian security officials and could not have been able to hide their identities too easily.

My main task on the project was to design the content of the OPC intervention and see to it that the workshop attained its objectives. I asked for and was given the necessary key information about the militant group. The information made available to me was more than I needed. Some part of it therefore went into my "reserve". I did the same thing before the Oke-Ogun intervention started.

The issues focused on during the Oke-Ogun and Akure interventions were almost the same. Our basic goal was to transform positively how the OPC members perceive and violently react to the conflicts around them. We wanted the OPC movement, if it had to be in existence at all, to be an asset to the building of democratic political systems in Nigeria rather than a liability, which it was gradually turning itself into. The training programmes therefore involved getting the trainees to understand that a conflict is not necessarily dysfunctional; it could have some positive outcomes. What comes out of a conflict is presented to the participants as a logical product of how the conflict is handled by the parties. If handled negatively, then the conflict produces a destructive outcome; if handled constructively, the conflict produces a positive outcome. The workshop's participants were introduced to the role of perceptions in conflict escalation and made to see why and how their perceptions of others could be adjusted positively. They were taught and made to practice communication, facilitation, negotiation, conciliation and mediation skills. The workshops were discussion-driven and each of the activities involved role-plays and simulation exercises. There were several group workshops. All these promoted active participation. The OPC members opened up about the problems they have with the Nigerian state, the Hausa-Fulani, and why they resorted to political violence. In all, they extricated themselves from the tag of a "criminal movement" given to the OPC by the federal government of Nigeria.

The methods used during the workshops for collecting our data include participant (and non-participant) observation, group discussion and personal interviews. The three enabled us to gain mastery over the meanings, categories, and language of the militant movement. The interaction between the OPC members and us was made quite meaningful because of the length of time we spent together. For about six weeks (for the two projects) all of us slept in the same hotel, ate together and exchanged information freely. During this period, the OPC members held their regular meetings; they sang their solidarity songs as they usually do in their natural settings; they prayed and carried out "preventive rituals". To enable me to plug into the ongoing world of natural communication of the militants, I spent several hours with them every evening at the bar of the hotels that we used, the surest place to find many of them. During this period of having to "hang around", I became more deeply immersed in the communicative behaviour of the OPC boys. As Irwin (1972: 118) noted, "structures and meanings that order a group's activities are constituted by their statements to each other – that is, by their on-going descriptions, discussions and disputes". In addition to gaining insight into the personality of the members, I learnt a lot about the past, present, and future goals of the movement and found the boys to be more informed about the goings-on in Nigeria than the ordinary Nigerian assumes. I learnt a lot about the group's ideology – those aspects that are negotiable and those that are not negotiable. I also found the group to have more profound grass-roots support than the Nigerian state is aware of.

Several group discussions were deliberately built into the training programmes. The discussions enabled each member of the movement to align their individual version of what "really happened" with those of other members. The group discussion enabled the researcher to enter into and participate in the world of the OPC. I learned from both the verbal and non-verbal cues of the members; I became more familiar with how the group constructs its social reality. It was possible to probe some obscure areas, and gauge the mood of individual members as the discussion changed from one issue to the other. I was particularly fascinated with how the groups reached agreement on controversial issues. More lessons were learnt from the non-verbal activities: their shared delusions, cues suggesting what "damage" the group could still do, and cues suggesting that certain national questions in Nigeria have to be addressed immediately. They became emotional and spoke in pitched tones when certain sets of national questions in Nigeria are raised. They became irritated when the name of the Hausa-Fulani ethnic group was mentioned along with the others in the country.

Irwin (1972: 127) advised that a researcher sourcing data (from deviant groups), using group discussion method:

must be particularly careful that he does not offend people. He must never appear belligerent or overbearing, for this will damage his relationships with most people and stop the flow of information. He must attempt to probe and pursue elusive material, and to provoke discussions and arguments over aspects of the criminal life, with extreme tact and agility.

We took this advice to heart and were able to sustain the friendship of the OPC members throughout the projects reported here and even beyond it.

At the end of each day's work, some members of the organization came to my room to share more information with me – most especially issues that some of them did not feel safe enough to discuss in the "open meeting". I benefited immensely from the interactions. Proceedings of the workshops are recorded on videotapes, while the information obtained from interviews and informal group discussions are written in a notebook. I recorded my data on a daily basis – sometimes at night when the activities of the day were considered to have been concluded.

Ethical considerations

The details of the data gathered in the course of the above projects are not reported in this chapter. Our interest here is restricted to reporting how the data was collected. We cannot report our findings here, because we do not have the permission of the OPC to do so. We intend to seek such permission in the future when a full-blown study of the movement will be conducted.

One could study a group or issue for a variety of reasons. The research could be for gathering data necessary for policy formation, or it could be for academic purposes or for both purposes. My main reason for getting involved in the projects reported above was to provide the OPC members with skills that could reduce their inclination towards political violence. We decided to do this as a way of creating the necessary peaceful environment for turning Nigeria into a great nation-state in which the constituent members peacefully co-exist.

I came before the OPC members, in the two projects reported above, as a social worker and not as an academic investigator. Neither USAID/ OTI nor the OPC were formally informed about my academic interest in the militia movement. None of them is probably aware that I gathered so much "private information" about the group. The OPC members might consider my action a betrayal of trust should I begin to make public reference to the "private discussions" they had with me during the OTI projects. To this extent, it might not be ethical for me at this stage to begin to report some of the things I was told either at Iseyin (for the Oke-Ogun project) or Akure. This partly explains why this chapter focuses on "methods" but is silent on "findings".

Beyond what the OPC members might feel, we can also pose the question: "Is it morally right for me to use the information that I gathered for academic purposes?" I am most likely to have both "No" and "Yes" answers. "No" because of the accepted ethical standard in sociological and anthropological studies that it is always necessary for researchers to get the permission of their informants before having the information collected from them published. The "Yes" answer will come from researchers who believe that if medical doctors, working in medical schools, could publish information obtained from their patients without obtaining any permission, then I too could publish the kind of information that I have collected. The work of a conflict management practitioner, like that of a social worker, is comparable to that of a medical doctor in the sense that they are all working towards reducing social problems. We can however look at the issue from another perspective and arrive at a "No" answer. Whereas the medical doctor only reports the disease that afflicted the patient, a conflict management practitioner in my situation will at best focus a report on actors more than actions in the movement. My report would therefore have required my "naming names". This might not be fair on the people reported.

Having successfully worked with the OTI from 2000 to 2002, I could lay claim to a good knowledge of the modus operandi of USAID/OTI. The organization would not have raised any objection if I suggested doing a write-up on the OPC. OTI would have even given me the necessary financial support to go ahead with the project. I am saying this because of the financial support that I got from the organization to work on two books (Albert, 2001a, Albert, 2001b). The first focuses on some of the intervention methods used in the OTI projects in Nigeria; the second focuses on some "success stories" from the communities in which the organization worked. The OPC issue could have been included as a chapter in the second book (Albert, 2001b) but for the touchy nature of the matter in contemporary Nigerian society. The projects we carried out are to help reduce violence in the Nigerian society and, by so doing, make our own contribution to consolidating sustainable development in the country. Those who are not careful enough to gather all the necessary details of the intervention might regard us as supporters of the movement.

Some colleagues might also want to challenge the reliability of the data collected from the Oke-Ogun and Akure projects. The setting was "not natural" and this could have affected some of the things I observed or was told. The OPC members were removed from their natural setting and brought to the two locations. They knew quite well, what the workshops were all about: to dialogue on how to make the OPC become a non-violent organization. Some members of the group might have simply put up a bogus front considered appropriate for the setting. This is a possibility. I wonder though if "everybody" and "at all the time" could have succeeded so well to put up a bogus front at such workshops. Nobody was forced at the meeting to say anything. They did however see the need to "open up". The OPC members were honest in their dealings with us. We could see this very clearly. This derived largely from the interactive and experiential learning methods that we used at the workshops. The focus discussion forums built into the workshop sessions could not have allowed everybody to put up a "bogus front" at the same time.

In all, we can say with boldness that the data collected from the two projects discussed above are very useful, especially when analysed against the background of the various official claims, newspaper and magazine reports, and petitions on the OPC saga in Nigeria. We are however not saying that we have collected enough information about the movement; the work is, in fact, just starting. Our level of attainment, so far, constitutes just a first step in our drive to know the OPC better. The little that we know, for now, could be used to prepare questions and questionnaires to be used in future projects. The field methods used in this paper can be used for reaching and studying some other ethnic militia groups around the world.

REFERENCES

Albert, Isaac Olawale (2001a) *Introduction to Third-Party Intervention in Community Conflicts*, Ibadan: PETRAF/John Archers Publishers.
———— ed. (2001b) *Building Peace, Advancing Democracy: Experience with Third-Party Intervention in Nigeria's Conflicts*, Ibadan: PETRAF/John Archers Publishers.
Albert, Isaac Olawale, Olaoba O.B., and Adekola, O.O. (2001) *Ethnic Groups and Conflicts in Nigeria, Volume 5: The Southwest Zone of Nigeria*, Ibadan: Programme on Ethnic and Federal Studies.
Amuwo, Kunle, Bach, Daniel C., and Lebeau, Yanneds (2001) *Nigeria During The Abash Years (1993–1998)*, Ibadan: IFRA.
Azarya, Victor (1988) "Recording State–Society Relations: Incorporation and Disengagement", in Donald Rothchild and Naomi Chazan, eds., *The Precarious Balance: State and Society in Africa*, Boulder, Colo: Westview Press.
Azarya, Victor and Chazan, Naomi (1987) "Disengagement from the State in Africa: Reflections on the Experience of Ghana and Guinea", *Comparative Studies in Society and History* 29(1).
Bayart, Jean François (1999) *The Criminalization of the State in Africa*, Oxford: International African Institute in Association with James Curry.
Bell, Daniel, ed. (1964) *The Radical Right*, New York: Doubleday.
Bell, J. Bowyer (1975) *Transnational Terror*, Washington, DC/Stanford, CA: American Enterprise Institute for Public Policy Research/Hoover Institution of War, Revolution and Peace, Stanford University.
Bouchier, David (1982) "Review of 'The Voice and the Eye' by Alain Touraine", *British Journal of Sociology* 33: 296–7.
Cohen, Joshua (1985) "Strategy or identity: New theoretical paradigms and contemporary social movements", *Social Research* 52(4): 663–716.
Devore, Wynetta and Schlesinger, Elfriede G. (1981) *Ethnic-Sensitive Social Work Practice*, St. Louis, Toronto, and London: C.V. Mosby.

Dobash, Rebecca Emerson and Dobash, Russell P. (1992) *Women, Violence and Social Change*, London: Routledge.

Du Toit, Pierre (1995) *State Building and Democracy in Southern Africa, Botswana and South Africa*, Washington DC: United States Institute of Peace Press.

Feldman, Allen (1995) "Ethnographic states of emergency", in Carolyn Nordstrom and Antonius C.G.M. Robben, eds., *Fieldwork Under Fire: Contemporary Studies of Violence and Survival*, Berkeley, Los Angeles, and London: University of California Press, pp. 224–252.

Fourchard, Laurent (2001) "Editorial", *IFRA Ibadan: Newsletter of the French Institute for Research in Africa*, X(2).

Germain, Carel Bailey, ed. (1979) *Social Work Practice: People and Environments*, New York: Columbia University Press.

Glaser, Barney G. (1967) *The Discovery of Grounded Theory*, Chicago: Aldine.

Green, Linda (1995) "Living in a state of fear", in Carolyn Nordstrom and Antonius C.G.M. Robben, eds., *Fieldwork Under Fire: Contemporary Studies of Violence and Survival*, Berkeley, Los Angeles and London: University of California Press, pp. 105–127.

Gubrium, Jaber F. and Silverman, David, eds. (1989) *The Politics of Field Research*, London: Sage.

Haynes, Jeffrey (1997) *Democracy and Civil Society in the Third World: Politics and New Social Movements*, Cambridge: Polity Press.

Kingston, Paul and Penhale, Bridget, eds. (1995) *Family Violence and the Caring Professions*, Houndmills: Macmillan.

Irwin, Jay (1972) "Participant-observation of criminals", in Jack D. Douglas, ed., *Research on Deviance*, New York: Random House.

Langan, Mary and Day, Lesley (1992) *Women, Oppression and Social Work*, London: Routledge.

Nechayev, Sergei (1869) *Revolutionary Catechism*, quoted in David C. Rapoport (1971) *Assassination and Terrorism*, Toronto: Canadian Broadcasting Corporation.

Nordstrom, Carolyn and Robben, Antonius C.G.M., eds. (1995) *Fieldwork Under Fire: Contemporary Studies of Violence and Survival*, Berkeley, Los Angeles and London: University of California Press.

Ogunsanya, Mobolaji and Popo-ola, S.O. (2001) "Intervention in the conflict between the Yoruba farmers and Fulani herdsmen in Oke-Ogun, Oyo State", in Isaac Olawale Albert, ed., *Building Peace, Advancing Democracy: Experience with Third-Party Interventions in Nigeria's Conflicts*, Ibadan: PETRAF/ John Archers, pp. 86–100.

Osaghae, Eghosa (1998) *Crippled Giant: Nigeria Since Independence*, London: Hurst.

——— (1999) "Exiting from the state in Nigeria", *African Journal of Political Science* 4(1): 83–98.

Phillipson, C. (1992) "Confronting elder abuse", *Generations Review* 2(3): 2–3.

Pincus, Allen and Minahan, Anne (1973) *Social Work Practice: Model and Method*, Ithaca, IL: FE Peacock.

Punch, Maurice (1993) "Observation and the police: the research experience", in Martyn Hammersley, ed., *Social Research: Philosophy, Politics and Practice*, London: Sage Publications/Open University.

Rapoport, David C. (1971) *Assassination and Terrorism*, Toronto: Canadian Broadcasting Corporation.

Robben, Antonius C.G.M. (1995) "Seduction and Persuasion: The politics of truth and emotion among victims and perpetrators of violence", in Carolyn Nordstrom and Antonius C.G.M. Robben, eds., *Fieldwork Under Fire: Contemporary Studies of Violence and Survival*, Berkeley, Los Angeles and London: University of California Press, pp. 81–103.

Robben, Antonius C.G.M. and Nordstrom, Carolyn (1995) "Introduction: The Anthropology and Ethnography of Violence and Sociopolitical Conflict", in Carolyn Nordstrom and Antonius C.G.M. Robben, eds., *Fieldwork Under Fire: Contemporary Studies of Violence and Survival*, Berkeley, Los Angeles and London: University of California Press, pp. 1–23.

Rosenbaum, Hans Jon and Sederberg, Peter C., eds. (1976) *Vigilante Politics: Absorbing Study of a Dangerous Shortcut: Order without Law*, Philadelphia: University of Pennsylvania Press.

Rotimi, A. Ola and Ihonvbere, Julius (1994) "Democratic Impasse: Remilitarization in Nigeria", *Third World Quarterly* 15(4): 669–689.

Rubin, Herbert J. and Rubin I.S. (1995) *Qualitative Interviewing: The Art of Hearing Data*, Thousand Oaks, London and New Delhi: Sage Publications.

Siporin, Max (1975) *Introduction to Social Work Practice*, New York: Macmillan.

Sluka, Jeffrey A. (1995) "Reflections on managing danger in fieldwork: dangerous anthropology in Belfast", in Carolyn Nordstrom and Antonius C.G.M. Robben, eds., *Fieldwork Under Fire: Contemporary Studies of Violence and Survival*, Berkeley, Los Angeles and London: University of California Press, pp. 276–294.

Touraine, Alan (1971) *The Post-Industrial Society*, London: Wildwood House.

—— (1983) *Anti-Nuclear Protest*, Cambridge: Cambridge University Press.

Turner, Francis J. (1974) "Some considerations on the place of theory in current social work practice", in Francis J. Turner, ed., *Social Work Treatment*, New York: Free Press.

—— (1978) *Psychosocial Therapy*, New York: Free Press.

6

Researching ethno-political conflicts and violence in the Democratic Republic of Congo

Arsène Mwaka Bwenge

Just as successive volcanic eruptions and earthquakes threaten to destroy the towns and settlements of the eastern part of the Democratic Republic of Congo (DRC) (Provinces Nord-Kivu and Sud-Kivu), the frequent tremors within the country's social fabric poses a further threat. Kivu was a base for rebel groups in the 1990s. Ethno-political conflicts and tensions have been kept simmering for a long time by the Mobutu regime's supposed rationalization of politics and progress through the major projects of the nation-state and one-party set-up from 1965–1997. The democratization process of the 1990s was meant to bring about "authentic nationalism" and "national unity" and do away with "tribalism and regionalism", but in fact it led to social implosion and gave free rein to power struggles which brought about crises of identity, and crises in economics and politics at local, national, regional, and even international levels.

Indeed, since 1992, indigenous ethnic groups in the province of Katanga (the Lunda, Lubakat, Bemba, Lamba, and Hemba) have experienced widespread "ethnic cleansing" in acts of violence between diverse ethnic groups, driving the Luba-Kasaï and assimilated groups (Songye, Kanyoka, Lulu) out of the province. Also in 1992, the district of Ituri in the eastern province saw violent conflict that set the Lendu-Ngiti against the Hema. The conflicts continue to the present day and have spread to other ethnic groups such as the Bira and the Alur. In the mountainous provinces of Nord-Kivu (North Kivu) and Sud-Kivu (South Kivu), conflicts of an unusually violent nature have, on the one side, the Hunde,

Nyanga, Tembo, Nande, Shi, Rega, Bembe, Fuliiru, and Vira communities, who see themselves as indigenous, and, on the other side, the Hutu and Tutsi communities, seen as outsiders and foreigners (coming from Rwanda and Burundi). It should be emphasized here that these two ethnic groups are not homogenous, stable, and coherent. Inter- and intra-ethnic conflicts run through them and regularly cause splits. In each of these conflicts, the concept of an "essential identity" is a constant factor.

In his discussion of the anatomy of violence in Africa, Jean-Claude Willame (1972: 13–33) lists the most evident characteristics of "African angers" (an expression by the Cameroon essayist Célestin Monga). These include: the involvement and participation on a large scale of civilians in the conflicts; the proliferation of brutal and seemingly irrational violence; the trivialization of a fairly unsophisticated, but destructive armament; the fact that the various media take an active part in the conflicts; the long duration of civil wars; the massive displacement of populations with resultant refugee camps and displaced persons; the essential identity question; and the state of overload which the international system of conflict management has reached. With regard to the question of essential identity, Willame (1972: 25) argues that in the light of concepts such as "globalization" or "one world", the Westphalian state order is breaking up, but the multiform resurgence of this "identity order", which is not peculiar to Africa, makes it of special interest to the human sciences. Yet in the 1960s, identity was reduced to ethnicity, and in the African context, was studied only by a handful of French or Anglo-Saxon anthropologists.

Peacemakers need to understand the complex, multifarious nature of identity. While a great number of peacemaking studies and activities have been carried out in these regions, the result is paradoxical: the number of these studies increases in relation to the intensification of the violence. The studies may be scientific, but they do little to ease the violence. I argue that we need to rethink scientific practices and examine the methodological and ethical problems at stake. There are problems associated with data collection and with the scope of explanations, because normal theorizations and conceptualizations do not readily incorporate issues raised by ethnic conflict and violence. My main objective in this chapter is to list the methodological and ethical problems in the field of study in the DRC (principally in the eastern provinces), to identify their scope and examine their mechanisms and structures, with a view to setting up new methods and courses of action for studying ethnic conflict in Africa.

The chapter is divided into three principal sections. The first focuses on the challenges facing social sciences when dealing with the ethno-political conflicts and violence in the DRC. The second section considers the specific problems of data collection within the context of a society divided by violence. The third and final section casts a critical eye over some of the problems associated with the social organization of research and the scope of explanations.

The challenge to social sciences by ethno-political conflicts and violence in the DRC

A profile of ethnicity and violence in the DRC

The Democratic Republic of Congo has experienced conflicts and violence right from the first hours of its independence on 30 June 1960. The country experienced a political crisis, which manifested itself both through struggles between its rulers at the top, and through ethnic struggles at a local and provincial level (see Kabuya, n.d.). The fledgling process of democratization was rapidly reduced to the level of ethnic competition before spilling over into rebellions in the west and eastern regions (Libois, 1966; Verhaegen, 1966, 1969) and to secession by Kasaï and Katanga (Kabuya, 1986: 500; Sylla, 1977: 23). Kabuya (1986: 500) speaks of "national tribalism" to underline the paradox between the call to nationalism and recourse to those political strategies which carry in their wake ethnicity as "behaviour, negative attitude which creates in a given social milieu, a network of attraction and repulsion between the members of two or several groups which make up this social milieu".

The chaos and anarchy that followed on from this crisis was used officially to justify the coup d'état on 24 November 1964, which brought General Mobutu and his MPR (*Mouvement Populaire de la Révolution*; the Popular Revolutionary Movement) party into control of the country. In spite of all the slogans proclaiming nationalism as the philosophy behind the political management framework of the new one-party system, a resort to ethnicity and regionalism was implicitly in operation. This meant that from the launch of the process of democratization in April 1990, many conflicts that had been brewing under Mobutu's government exploded, principally taking on an ethnic shape. Contradictions between the forces for change and the "forces for the status quo" (the *Mouvance Présidentielle*, the President's circle of influence), were manifested as struggles between nationals from the provinces of eastern and western Kasaï (generically called Luba) under the leadership of Tshisekedi Etienne and those from the Zairean Equateur province with General Mobutu at their head. In addition, successive alliances in Katanga province in the south-east of the country, together with the social conflicts that prevailed due to unequal access to the commercial products necessary for industries, such as mining and the railways, led to widespread ethnic cleansing (see Mwaka Bwenge, 2001).

Similarly, the accelerated implosion of the state apparatus, which was already visible from the outset of the democratization process – and which was bound to accelerate due to what was at stake – gave free rein to sections of the population to express violently the problems of territory, power, and identification that had remained unresolved for so long. These expressions of violence have occurred since 1992 in the conflicts between the Lendu-Ngiti and Hema, and those in the provinces of North and South Kivu. It was these conflicts, crystallized by the conflagrations in Rwanda and Burundi, which led to the October 1996 war of the Alliance of Democratic Forces for the Liberation of Congo (Zaire), and the August 1998 war of the Congolese Assembly for Democracy in the DRC, and leaves the country still unsettled.

I have described the dialectical interactions between these conflicts from the local, national, regional, and international points of view, as well as the specific atypical forms they took, and these conflicts lay bare the methodological inadequacies within typical social science practices in the DRC.

From local to national, regional, and international levels: features of the current crisis

The current crisis in the DRC has mobilized social, political, and military forces on several levels. Some have gone so far as to identify it as a "first world war". There are more than five foreign armies, several national rebellions in neighbouring countries, a multitude of armed bands and militias and a significant number of mafia-type actors (Mwaka Bwenge, 2002). The characteristic elements cited above are present in addition to some particular developments that are rather unusual:

- The omnipresence of ethnic aspects to those conflicts that are said to be of national or regional interest.
- The emergence and growth of new mercenary groups with militias and other armed groups coming into contention.
- The cross-border nature of perpetrators of the violence, which produces an increase in conflagrations.
- The emergence of new splits and ethno-racist ideologies among the ethnic group, the Nile Bantus, leading to a redefinition of alliances and social and political-military relationships.
- The development of delinquent and criminal activities involving participants at local, national, regional, and international levels.

- The dividing up of the national territory into enclaves which become less and less under state control, or become "stateless", or under mafia-type control.
- The mainly militarist control of excessively politicized areas, which brings with it the violation of fundamental rights.
- The rise and activism of a civil society which is becoming more and more involved in violent conflicts and therefore in political power with its anticipated material gains.
- The direct implication of foreign powers in these conflicts, in violence and in the running of the Congolese territory.

Such a picture calls for extreme vigilance on the part of any researcher who needs to question the prevailing methodological system and theoretical approaches. Although social science research projects in the DRC aim to understand and explain the situation, the complexity of the current crisis and the difficulties in identifying its real cause with a view to peacemaking pose a significant challenge to the scientific community.

The collapse of the "republic of scientists": methodological and ethnic questions

As the current crisis in the DRC reaches its height; it reveals the limits of the "republic of scientists" and its methodological tools. Seeking to identify the position of ethnicity in the current conflicts, in which political, geo-political, geo-strategic, economic-mafia, and militarist issues are at stake, poses problems with both theoretical and methodological approaches. Indeed, theories abound in explanations for the causes of the conflicts. Amoo (1997: 3–14; see also Burton 1979 and 1990, from which Amoo draws inspiration), for example, suggests the following possible explanations:

- The multi-ethnic African state is fundamentally in conflict; stability demands therefore that "tribalism" is transcended by modernization.
- Poverty is the source of conflicts in Africa; the relief of poverty would provide, as it were, a panacea.
- Ethnicity and the conflicts resulting from it are an ideological creation of local extremists to serve their objectives, political and otherwise.
- The conflicts are a result of the ignorance or repression of the basic human socio-psychological needs which relate to growth and development: identity, security, recognition, participation, and autonomy.

While we can be sure that such approaches have not always brought about an understanding of conflicts in Africa, it is at least evident that the situation in the DRC demands deeper reflection. It presents an opportunity to question the whole process of research via the stages of data collection, understanding, and explanation.

Data collection and violence in the DRC: specific problems

The field of conflict and violence in the DRC presents a range of specific problems which must be identified. I intend to focus here on four: those based on the imaginary, those on witness accounts, those from media coverage and those from historical sources.

The imaginary: perceptions and beliefs as new catalysts within conflict situations

Preoccupation with objectivity often causes researchers to seek "objective facts" in order to explain ethno-political conflicts. This could be described as "the study of facts as if they were things". However, close observation of societies in eastern DRC brings an understanding that, within the context of violent conflicts, the beliefs about and the perception of the facts more than the facts themselves become the catalysts for conflict.

While the local problems in South Kivu (nationality, power, and territory) have been identified in many studies over more than ten years, the explanations of the various conflicts that have been observed remain insufficient. We can use as an example the events of 20 March 1993 in the locality of Ntoto (in Walikale) in North Kivu. The versions of the facts presented by each of the parties (Rwandan speakers on one side and Nyanga-Hunde on the other), revealed that the Rwandans had believed a rumour of an imminent attack by the Nyanga-Hunde. In the same way, civil disobedience started by the Hutu community in protest against the exclusion of its delegates from the national sovereign conference was perceived by the Nyanga-Hunde as a means of questioning the customary authority in the villages. It was these beliefs and perceptions that would serve as catalysts for the taking up of arms and the popular massacres which would follow.

A degree of return to ancient religious faith may also be observed within the population. It is in terms of prophecy, of dissatisfaction with and/or copying their ancestors, of the magic power of witch doctors, of Jehovah-God, of nature, and of the supernatural that certain events are experienced and reported by actors and witnesses. The mahi-mahi militia,[1] for example, are notoriously believed to be invulnerable as a result of a magic power that reduces enemy bullets to water. A repertoire of prohibitions and taboos can in this way justify an otherwise acknowledged vulnerability and thus sustains the myths, legends, and epics of such a group. To this religious feeling can also be added a whole gamut of prejudices, myths, stereotypes, and clichés prevalent in communities that are communicated via derisory remarks, songs, stories, and popular anecdotes. They prevent any lucid observation of the facts by the warring populations by helping to caricature the "other". Because they are experienced as an indisputable truth, they can be seen to constitute a genuine ideology (Sargent, 1990).

For some time, researchers have already denounced these elements as having repercussions on the pseudo-scientific observations inherited from the colonial period, similar to Bashizi's "Hamite myth". Bashizi emphasized that the first written works on the Great Lakes region conveyed certain pseudo-racist prejudices based on local myths, the political demands of colonialization, and the ignorance or inadequacy of observation (1981: 218–43). This was then perpetuated through social stratification and informed the splits in the Great Lakes conflicts: the Hima-Tutsi from the Nile, a superior "race" and "bringers of civilisation"; the Hutu (Bantu blacks and serfs "to be civilized"); and the Batwa (backward and primitive). Such prejudices and myths continue to be perpetuated to this day in social contacts and mobilized in moments of crisis, providing rationalizations for the protagonists.

It is within this context, that for the Rwandan-speaking Tutsi, for example, the Congolese are "good for nothings", merely "ghosts" (a shadow of a man and not men), unsophisticated and considered as "Hutu in serfdom". In contrast, for the Congolese, the Tutsi are sadists who weep over dead cows more than over dead men, and are "uncircumcised" (that is, physically weak), and so on. There is a Hunde proverb – "Utechi balume analya n'abarondo" (Only a man who does not know human beings could share a meal with the Rwandans) – which sums up popular feeling towards the Tutsi.

If it is admissible that ethnicity, just like any other feeling of identity (nationality, regionalism, or religion) gives rise to passions, emotions, instincts, and rancour, it should be recognized also that this is not often taken into account in observations which wish to be seen as scientific. However, it is sometimes within the heart of a people that the explanation for the perpetuation of conflict and antagonism is to be found. This constitutes a new challenge for social science if it is to enlarge the base of knowledge regarding human societies divided by conflict.

Silent violence: is the refusal to testify a new culture?

Events unravelled very quickly in Kivu: battles, punitive expeditions, vendettas, the pillaging of natural resources, and so on. But while it would seem that the reasons for this are already well-known – fighting between ethnic groups, between the state armed forces for nationality and political power, as well as for mining resources – when the question is asked: What is happening at this particular moment, who is doing what and why and how?, it is disappointing to find how little has been grasped by the international community.

Indeed, an echo resounds out of the horrific violence in the eastern part of the DRC. Very few things are known about this area, and for this reason, the abundant humanitarian and political peacemaking activity, as well as scientific work, takes place *alongside* the real causes of the protracted violence, particularly the absence of legitimate political institutions. The actors and first-hand witnesses in the conflicts in this region produce few or no documents at all, and refuse to testify about their experiences. They have very little or nothing to do with the notebooks, microphones, and cameras of researchers and journalists. Fascination with foreigners, even Westerners, no longer exists. The violence is silent. Are we witnessing the emergence of a new culture?

A two-pronged explanation can be put forward for this attitude, which is as prevalent in the countryside as it is in the cities and towns. Firstly, civil populations find themselves taken hostage by the different confronting factions: government parties and their allies, rebels and their allies, and the mahi-mahi and their allies. To testify in such a situation is to "betray"; it is advisable therefore to have a security policy. However, as there is no monopoly on the violence, it is unlikely that one can take security measures in the face of death, which is still the common fate of "traitors". This condemns numerous people to silence. If there are courageous people, they generally are recruited from the ranks of the NGOs, who accuse and denounce more than they describe and explain. There are even those (warlords, soldiers and militiamen) who often prefer to make accusations than to report events. It is within the aggressive context of the violation of human rights and legitimate democratic defence that the actors and witnesses who are not always impartial and detached formulate discussions on the conflicts.

Secondly, organizations that wish to remain secret (such as the mahi-mahi) not only cultivate terror among their own combatants in order to force them not to recount their experiences, but also prepare official press releases for external exposure. These statements often are built up around the taboos and myths of their ancestors, which subsequently render any attempt at penetrating an understanding of their actions even more difficult.

So, the major objective for social science researchers in any new approach that claims to be critical must be to get to know the real actors in the violent conflicts in eastern DRC. This requirement includes getting to know their real objectives outside of the "official press releases"; the local, regional, and international dialectical interactions; and to understand more substantially the realities of so-called delinquent, criminal, and mafia activities at the heart of the rampant violence we assume we know.

A new trap: media coverage

Political sociology has shown that the fact that a population is denied the chance to testify publicly about the negative character of the events they have experienced, and that communication channels are inaccessible to statements of protest, does not mean that that population has actually been silent. Rather, they express themselves in "languages, accounts, statements which you need to know how to decode" (Mbembe, 1988: 210). The content of these communications is not necessarily that of resistance to oppression nor is it of revolution. It is sometimes a simple description or, paradoxically, an expression of support. As Mbembe says: "all that comes from the people is not necessarily revolutionary" (1988: 210).

However, in the absence of "obvious" and "classical" statements, reports by the local press and radio stations, and by human rights and environmental activists, development agencies, pastors, priests, and human aid agencies, are taken as the means of expression by the eye-witness population. In a society torn apart by conflicts, these channels of communication are taken over by the dominant actors, thereby ensuring the main messages are under the control of the protagonists. For this reason, they frequently become the means of expression of the opinions and "facts" of the protagonist elites; they become another weapon in their arsenal. However, each of the agencies believes that it is the "true spokesperson" for what is called the "people". The majority say they speak for civil society and that the messages purporting to emanate from the "people" are always violent or accusatory. Very often popular opinion is actually the opposite.

In the DRC, the present situation is not far from that in Rwanda in 1994 when the media, instead of giving out news information, issued orders, indoctrinated the population, and incited violence and ethnic hatred. This can be seen by the Catholic-controlled media in zones under the control of the two rebel wings of the Congolese Assembly for Democracy (RCD), a platform of politicians and others in civil society who are fighting to dismantle Kabila's dictatorship and establish a democratic regime founded on popular legitimacy. In its evening broadcasts presented by "Rastamen" Muyahudi Mandove and Issa Wetu,

Radio Moto in the Butembo-Beni diocese attacked the adversaries of its choice in coded language (Tutsi), while clearly expressing sympathy to the local mahi-mahi militias. In this area, how information is treated depends more frequently on the choices and political leanings of the bishop than on reality.

A second example of the media trap is that of the two famous newspapers for the region under rebel control: *Les Coulisses* (Behind the Scenes) and *Le Millénaire* (Millennium). In the leadership struggles that have split the Kisangani wing of the RDC for a long time, the former paper, whose editor Nicaise Kibel Bel Oka is from the Bakongo cultural area, supports or gives a version of the facts which favours Professor Ernest Wamba Dia Wamba, President of the RCD/Kisangani (RCD/ ML), who is also of Bakongan origin. The latter newspaper, meanwhile, edited by Joska Kaninda, supports Antipas Mbusa Nyamwisi. However, support can be only a step away from distortion and exaggeration.

In addition to local media, international media agencies such as Voice of America (VOA), the BBC, *Radio France Internationale* (RFI), *Canal Afrique*, and *Africa n° 1* also have large audiences. The control of information has become more complicated with new communications technology (such as Satphone, Iridium, the Internet), and outright lies, exaggeration, and orders have been communicated by false representatives of combatant groups. In the first six months of 2001, for example, in its *Central Africa Today* broadcast, a John Baumbili, who pretended to be calling from the Semliki Valley in North Kivu in the name of a non-existent mahi-mahi group, regularly called VOA via satellite phone. However, this young lawyer from the city of Beni was simply calling from his home to scoff at the rebel authorities of RCD-ML (Congolese Rally for Democracy – Liberation Movement) in Kisangani.

In fact, media coverage of the conflicts in eastern DRC is full of traps for researchers. "Media of hatred and death", or "Unethical and partisan media", or "Media encouraging resistance, combat and a call to arms" – all these are qualifying terms used by those who wish to "make a moral statement" on this field with reference to the lessons and experiences to be drawn from the "genocide media" in Rwanda. For social scientific research, what remains necessary is a permanently critical eye, prudence, and a constant monitoring of the information supplied by those forms of media – which have in reality become a weapon of the protagonists rather than straightforward sources of information. These sources of information accuse more than describe, denounce more than they analyse and explain, and pass judgement more than they propose a way out. Researchers need to undertake a deep reflection on the use and abuse of these sources of information.

How to erase sources of history: "Old Wise Men", archives, and other documents as targets for the protagonists

The protagonists in the conflicts in eastern DRC, as we have emphasized above, want to control the output of information and comment on their activities. Taken to its conclusion, this knowledge leads us to assess certain sources of stories in these conflicts.

So, the "old wise men", as they are called locally (who are assumed to be the custodians of the historical knowledge of certain territorial disputes between communities and the ancient archivists of both colonial and post-colonial years and of all the other documents which give no succour to the theses held by one or other party in the disputes over property, nationality or local power) become the target of the protagonists. The general practice is the physical elimination of certain people (especially the tribal chiefs and the intellectual Hunde, Nyanga Nande and Shi elite in the conflicts over nationality and territory in Masisi in North Kivu), the burning of administration offices in villages and towns, and the checking and destroying of all other documents which are deemed to compromise the dominant group. The assassinations of Hunde tribal chiefs such as Mutoka, Mushakuli, Mashona, Mahire and Banduwabo in the violence of the 1990s are generally cited to illustrate this type of selective "intelligent" violence.

These orgies of violence, which cause the wrecking, burning, and massacring of all in their path, lead not only to the scarcity of the real human and written sources of information, but also to those that do exist being falsified and destroyed as a result of bad preservation. In the case of colonial archives, several researchers believe it necessary to resort to those kept in Belgium and elsewhere in the West. As for those of the post-colonial period, the question remains unanswered: How do you restore the history of conflicts in the 1960s, of the Mobutu regime, of the Kabila (the champion of "oral improvised administration") regime and of rebellions by those aware of probable future legal proceedings and who filter any written acts? How do you arrive at a version of the facts that is close to reality?

A clear response to these questions can result in furthering the resolution of the ethno-political conflicts in the eastern part of the DRC. By its nature, such a perspective can enrich the approach to conflicts in Africa and worldwide.

Critique of the social organization of research

The social organization of research cannot escape from political and social conflicts. Social scientists do not sit above the social and political hurly-burly; but at the same time their science does not come down to the ideology of the opposing actors (Touraine, 1973: 100–1). Over and above this issue, however, there is the problem of the awareness of, and even the "construction" of, social facts by the actors. This presents an ongoing debate on reciprocal relationships between social scientist and actor with regard to the conceptualization of legitimate research, the construction of models, and the role and function of research in society.

The "Scientist as God" against the "Ignorant Actor": a recurring question

The problem of distance between subject and object, and between researcher and actor, poses a recurring question. The whole evolution of the social sciences is marked by this debate which is approached from different angles: objectivity versus subjectivity, detachment, "the distant eye of the researcher", and so on. In trying to solve this problem of methodological distance, there is a danger that this could lead to studying "social facts as if they were things". Even worse, there is a danger that this could lead to human beings and societies being deprived of their voice by studying them using the model of the "pure sciences" (Borella, 1990: 153), those that study nature. If, in effect, society keeps silent about the need for research, then the social scientist may also keep silent and social sciences will no longer exist. It is therefore a monumental mistake to imagine social sciences within the relationships of a natural science model that proceeds by induction, generalization, and explanation. Rather, social science is located in the interrelationships between human beings.

A superficial observation of the field of study in the ethno-political conflicts in the Democratic Republic of Congo shows an "anti-social sciences attitude": that the researcher most commonly is the "scientist as God" as the "Great Lakes specialist" who engages in research while ignoring the real actors and their societies. The type of research currently in vogue consists of settling for documents (such as articles in newspapers or NGO reports), which are produced generally by the elite "situation retrievers" whose logic and interests the researchers do not know.

My contact with certain warring parties in the DRC conflicts has allowed me to see that individually and collectively they are aware of themselves, and that they are also aware of their actions and retain the meaning and motivation for them. Borella puts it best: "It is society itself, by its rules, its values, its practices which constructs the fact and not the researcher" (1990: 153). "Fact" is constructed by the researcher on the basis of a theoretical elaboration only if he or she intends to break with

explicit social institutions and practices, and consists therefore of information which is not immediately verifiable.

It is advisable, however, to put this stance into perspective. The
"popularization" of certain theories and research results also affects
the "popular constructions of the facts". It is advisable therefore for
researchers to establish their relationships with actors within a dialectical
interaction in order to make scientific progress. The researcher is not a
magician who can get to know society without actually participating
in social networks, and the actor is not as ignorant of his or her own practices as some of today's scientific methodologies in the DRC would have
us believe.

Loaded concepts and terms: should words be exorcised?

The social act is first of all an act of communication, and therefore of
representation, which is only possible through language. If language
seems to pose few problems for natural and life sciences – because scientific knowledge is expressed in formal, constructed language, it is a more
complex issue for the social sciences. For a long time, verifying how
appropriate language is to reality and assessing how adequate language
and thought is to various forms of language itself, has preoccupied the
philosophy of language (Soulez, 1985: 368). In the same way, intuitive
and immediate socio-political knowledge that would lay bare the social
aspects of communities does not exist. It is by means of conceptualization
that the knowledge is revealed. However, concepts themselves do not
guarantee unanimity in the social sciences.

When dealing with the ethno-political conflicts in the DRC, we can add
to these problems of a general nature for socio-political research the
affective, emotional, politicking, and romantic burden which accompanies
the concepts and terms in the production of knowledge. Concepts and
expressions such as tribe, autochtonous (native), allochtonous (foreign),
nationals, foreigners, Rwandan speakers, Rwandan Kimyarwanda-
speaking populations, registered, indigenous, Congolese, all of which are
used in the conflicts to identify the combatants, imply taking a stance,
making a judgement, or engaging politically through the meaning given
to them by the protagonists of conflicts in Kivu.

To illustrate, the sense of "autochthony", as it is understood by the
Hunde, Nyanga, Nande, Shi, Rega, Tembo, and Bembe, implies abori-
ginal Congolese who hold natural rights over the lands of their ancestors
which are in danger of being occupied by those whom they deem to
be "allochthonous" – foreigners (that is to say, non-nationals as they
understand it). Autochthony therefore is experienced as a tribal group-
ing based on blood in contrast to those who are called foreigners –

"Rwandans by blood". This situation has forced this latter group to invent defensive ethnic names such as Banyabwisha, Banyamulenge, Banyavyura, and Kinyarwanda-speaking Congolese populations in their quest for nationality. The neologisms laden with political motivation have been widely circulated and naively and/or unconsciously taken up by numerous researchers and other peace activists. Simple words therefore can trap researchers and, in doing so, can drive away all hopes for peace, as simple unwise usage of such concepts by the "peacemakers" is enough to intensify the violence. Should, then, existing concepts, terms, and expressions be exorcised or should new ones be invented?

This agonising interrogation can only find a means of resolution via a preliminary analysis without the compliance of the tools of research, with a constant epistemological vigilance right through the research process and a proven sense of prudence, all characteristics of a methodological approach appropriate to the particular features which the case of the DRC in particular, and of Central Africa in general, present. A critical introduction to the local vocabulary with its whole emotional and militant weight is required for a successful outcome for the researcher.

Schematic theorizations and ideologies

Literature on the ethno-political conflicts in the DRC reveals two principal tendencies on the part of the authors. On the one hand are those authors who write from inside Congo and who often are actors directly involved in the conflicts in question (Kabuya, 1997; Kambere, 1999a, Kambere, 1999b; Kanyama Chumbi, 1992; Mutambo, 1997; Ndeshyo, 1992; Rwakabuba, 1995; Vangu, 2000). On the other hand, there are European authors with an interest in African affairs who in most cases, write from outside Congo (Mungangu, 1999; Pabanel, 1991; Reyntjens and Marysse, 1996; Willame, 1997).[2]

According to the first group, the eastern DRC is in flames as a result of conflicts over nationality and territory between the Hunde, Nande, Nyanga, Bembe, Shi, Raga, and Tembo, who consider themselves to be the sole natives of the Kivu provinces, and the Hutu and Tutsi who consider themselves also native and/or as immigrants who have acquired Congolese nationality. Thus Kivu is presented as being a boxing ring where a face-to-face confrontation occurs between the "homogenous, stable forces" of the insiders against the outsiders. For this reason, the internal struggles within these forces, which are more artificial than real, are kept silent, ignored, and minimized at the expense of explanatory schemas which are thenceforth "conventional and official". In the same way, the second group of authors, by relying on documents which are open to question, most often artificially and decisively split the society into two.

Preoccupations which consist in determining which of the two groups of protagonists are right or wrong fall into "theorizations" which do not take their starting point from the actual political conflict, but rather from a cocktail of facts, wishes, interests, opinions, perceptions, and politicking claims, as well as from explanatory models of neighbouring or distant conflicts. In this way, for example, by splitting society into two, one is conforming to Rwandan and Middle Eastern logic, which promotes the idea that there are Nile-dwelling Hima-Tutsi and Bantu Hutu or Jews and Palestinians. Kivu societies are not as dualized as they are presented; alliances and splits can be seen between groups that some people describe as "against nature". Societies in the eastern provinces inevitably are perceived as being made up of communities that are naturally and at all costs opposed to each other. Any serious study should dwell on these considerations, grasp the whole dynamic and range and only then identify the true causes of the bloody conflicts in this region.

This "blind" attitude of researchers generally results in a priori conclusions and the filtering of data. What is essential for some of these studies if their theses are to be upheld is that supporting arguments should strengthen their claims. In not always doing so, the result is that exaggeration of the facts, lies, and denunciations of false plots of collective extermination come to the rescue of explanatory models which do not square with reality. These then become instruments of combat that serve to increase the intensity of conflicts rather than to make peace.

Research as an ideological binding and "code of good conduct"

The popularization of the research results described above affects popular reading practices and perceptions in everyday life. However, the reports of the intellectual, political, social, and ecclesiastical elites convey least the life of the general population; rather they act as a measure of the socio-political, economic conduct of the protagonist populations. They feed the conflicts in such a way that social relationships between individuals and communities are regulated more by ideals, clichés, prejudices, and perceptions – in other words by the ideologies which they convey. The result is that public opinion quickly forms classifications on the basis of these pseudo-scientific discourses: you are either pro-Rwandan or pro-native. This unsettles the "ideological authors". Speaking out against the notion of Congolese identity assumed by the Hutu residents of the DRC, Kambere (1999a: 24) paraphrased an Algerian journalist in this dilemma:

If you do speak out, you die
If you don't speak out, you die
Well, then, speak out and die.

Writings, therefore, are the continuation of the battlefield. Locally, in the eastern provinces, they are called "another front" because people know that writings inform the actions of the central government actors, the humanitarian crowd, and the peacemakers.

The publication of a new work is welcomed and exploited (whatever the origin of its author) in terms of new arguments for combat. The Catholic Faculties in Kinshasa, for example, who regularly organize colloquia and conferences on this theme, remain one of the fields of observation on the ramblings of the "reader-combatants" of these types of works. Also, it is not uncommon, on returning to the region, to re-encounter interviewees who repeat a story they have already told you, but in a version reworked by another author, rather than retracing the course of events as they happened. This poses real questions regarding researchers' methodological and ethical approaches from every angle. It is therefore advisable for researchers to look for solutions in such a way that respects varied methodological and ethical principles.

Conclusion: future directions

Scientific research does not only consist of meditating on an already observed reality; it consists above all in discovering the reality which is still hidden, still not properly observed, or which has never been observed, in general, not even suspected (Fourastie, 1966: 154).

It seems that the eastern region of the DRC is well-known to researchers focusing on ethnic conflict; however the precipitation of events, the rarity of witness accounts and of documents which rigorously relate the actions of those involved, the monopolizing of speech by the "combating elites" and the manipulation of history, all have resulted in research and peace-making activities which are far removed from an understanding of the prevailing problems. It is evident that if current negotiations via inter-Congolese dialogue bring peace to the geographic "top half" of the country, the contradictions of the "lower half" would remain intact and could even get worse. The withdrawal of aggressor countries and "power sharing" between the combatants in the DRC will likely be followed with violence and banditry in mountainous Kivu.

Such a pessimistic hypothesis brings the collapse of current academic thinking to light and leads to conjecture on the range of methods and practices. However, this brief conclusion may not be the appropriate place to undertake this critical revision. Here we are quite simply going to show some methodological and ethical paths. They revolve around a call to a re-reading of the fundamentals and principles of the so-called method of immediate history by the Belgian Professor Benoît Verhaegen (1969, 1974, 1983, 1994). Indeed, when he arrived in the DRC to teach sociology in the turbulent years of decolonization, Verhaegen noted the weakness of the prevailing methods – the functionalist paradigm – that recounted particularly fluid socio-political evolutions. Two facts rendered these methods and their principal documentary sources ineffective: the precipitation of events and the ideological orientation of the abundant colonial documentation which most of all described order, stability, and the instruments and aims of power, but did not give an account of the forces and ideologies of change. It therefore was necessary to make use of the "living techniques" – allowing the actors and witnesses involved in the change to speak – in order to grasp the whole dynamic of the Congolese crisis.

However, the concept of speaking out had scandalized a number of people for a long time as they equated it with spontaneous and intuitive expression. Verhaegen (1983) emphasized that such an act was intended within its epistemological meaning, placing the subject and object of the knowledge face-to-face without intermediaries; bringing the researcher physically and psychologically closer to the object of his or her research in order to construct their relationship by means of dialectical intersubjectivity. It was a question of facilitating relationships of reciprocal interaction and transformation by reducing the distance caused by language, ideologies, class status, gender, or the unequal role of each of the participants in an exchange of knowledge.

Now, more than a quarter of a century after Verhaegen launched the fundamentals of this method, I believe it is advisable to revisit it, not just for what it has meant up to now in terms of partisans and non-partisans, but in the light of new developments in African conflicts within the dynamics of globalization and its effects, of the new global, interlake and Central African geopolitics, of the internal restructuring/ recomposition of states, of the emergence of new cross-border, nonstate actors, and so on. With the possibility of an immediate history confirmed by numerous people (Sindjoun, 1999), anxieties are kept at the level of the "epistemological break" to be made in understanding the complexities of ethno-political conflicts. Further reflection on theorization needs to take place in the light of these complexities.

These are the markers from which we can envisage new paths: the increasing suppression of manipulative mediation, the ending of methodological delusions about the presumed ignorance of actors and witnesses;

the penetration of the banal, the derisory remarks and popular songs, the anecdotes, graffiti and other popular drawings, so as to understand that social acts are significant social practices and not inert things; the approaching of the facts at "grassroots", bringing documentation that is the result of face-to-face interaction with real actors and the general population, thus building up the trust of the latter. A more in-depth study can be devoted to this.

Notes

1. The mahi-mahi is an armed militia that has emerged from the violent ethno-political conflicts in mountainous Kivu since 1993. Initially called Ngilima, Katuku, Batiri, Vijana, the mahi-mahi are related to the ethnic groups who consider themselves indigenous to Kivu (Hunde, Nande, Nyanga, Shi, Rega, Bembe, Tembo). Officially, the mahi-mahi are opposed to the occupation of Kivu territory by the Hutu and Tutsi peoples who speak Kinyarwanda, who are considered to be of Rwandan nationality. However, the range of their actions nowadays exceeds these limits and involves several other issues of a political, ideological, cultural and economic nature (see Mwaka Bwenge 2002).
2. While this list is not exhaustive, it is nonetheless representative.

REFERENCES

Amoo, Sam K. (1997) *The Challenge of Ethnicity and Conflicts in Africa: The Necessity for a New Model*, New York: PNUD.

Anon (1962) *Will Masisi Always Remain Part of Nord-Kivu (North Kivu)?*, Bukavu: Congolese Presses, pp. 218–243.

Bashizi, Cirhagarhula (1981) "The Hamite myth, state formations and inter lake acculturation", in Anon., *The Ancient Civilisation of the Great Lakes Peoples*, Paris and Bujumbura: Karthala-CCB.

Borella, François (1990) *Critique of political knowledge*, Paris: Presses Universitaires de France.

Burton, John Wear (1979) *Deviance, Terrorism and War: The Process of Solving Unsolved Social and Political Problems*, New York: St. Martin's Press.

———— (1990) *Conflict; Resolution and Prevention*, New York: St. Martin's Press.

Fourastie, Jean (1966) *Conditions of the Scientific Spirit*, Paris: Gallimard.

Kabuya, Lumuna Sando (n.d.) *Nationalism? Tribalism? The Tribal Question in the Congo (Zaire)*, Brussels: Ed. Africa.

———— (1986) *Zairean Ideologies and Tribalism: The Paradoxical Revolution*, Louvain-la-neuve: Cabay.

———— (1997), *Conflicts in Eastern Zaire. Landmarks and Issues at Stake*, Kinshasa: Ed. Secco.

Kambere, Léonard Muhindo (1999a) *A Look at the Conflicts Among Nationalities in the Congo. Geo-historic Aspects*, Kinshasa: Ed. Yira.

—— (1999b) *A Look at the Conflicts Among Nationalities in the Congo. Legal Aspects*, Kinshasa: Ed. Yira.

—— (2000) *Quid les Hutu*, Kinshasa: Ed. Yira.

Kanyama Chumbi, R. (1992) *The Populations of Kivu and the Law on Nationality. A Real or False Problematic*, Kinshasa: Ed. Select.

Libois, Jules Gérard (1966) *Secession in Katanga*, Brussels, Leopoldville: CRISP-INEP.

Mbembe, Achille (1988) *Unquiet Africa, Christianity, Power and the State in the Post-colonial Society*, Paris: Karthala.

Mungangu, Severin (1999) "Nationality in mountainous Kivu", in Paul Mathieu and Jean-Claude Willame, eds., *Conflicts and Wars in Kivu and in the Great Lakes Region: Between Local Tensions and Regional Escalation*, Tervurer, Paris: African Institute-l'Harmattant, pp. 201–211.

Mutambo, Jason (1997) *The Banyamuleng*, Kinshasa: unpub.

Mwaka Bwenge, Arsène (2001) *Identity, Political Power and "Wars of Liberation"* in Democratic Republic of Congo, www.aaps.co.zw.

Mwaka Bwenge, Arsène (2002) *Attempt to Identify Rebellions, Militias and Armed Groups Involved in Current Violence in Democratic Republic of Congo*, Kinshasa: Centre for Political Studies (CEP)/University of Kinshasa.

Ndeshyo, Rurihose (1992) *The Nationality of the Zairean Kinyarwanda Speaking Population Under the Law of 19 June 1981*, Kinshasa: Ed. électronique ASYST.

Pabanel, Jean Pierre (1991) 'The nationality question in Kivu', in *Politique Africaine* 41, March, 32–40.

Reyntjens, Filip and Marysse, Stefaan (1996) *Conflicts in Kivu: Intercedents and Issues at Stake*, Anvers: Centre of Studies for the African Great Lakes Region.

Rwakabuba, Cyprien (1995) *Memories and Witness Accounts*, Kinshasa: Isata.

Sargent, Lyman Tower (1990) *Contemporary Political Ideologies: A Comparative Analysis*, California: Pacific Grove.

Sindjoun, Luc (1999) *The Passive Revolution in Cameroon: State, Society and Change*, Dakar: Codesria.

Soulez, Antonia (1985) *The Manifesto of the Circle of Vienna*, Paris: PUF.

Sylla, Lancine (1977) *Tribalism and the One Party System in Black Africa*, Abidjan and Paris: Ivory Coast National University/Political Sciences Press Foundation.

Touraine, Alan (1973) *Production of Society*, Paris: Ed. du Seuil.

Vangu, Mambweni ma Busana (2000) *Premeditated Wars in the Region of the African Great Lakes: The Roles and Tentacles of the Tutsi International Power in DRC*, Kinshasa: Media for Peace.

Verhaegen, Benoît (1966) *Rebellions in the Congo*, Vol. I, Brussels, Leopoldville: IRES-CRISP-INEP.

Verhaegen, Benoît (1969) *Rebellions in the Congo*, Vol. II, Kinshasa: CRISP-IRES.

—— (1974) *Introduction to Immediate History*, Gembloux: Duculot.

—— (1983) *The Immediate History Method and its Application in Africa*, unpublished.

——— (1994) "Principles and practice of immediate history in Africa", in Jean Tshonda Omasombo, ed., (1994) *Zaire Under the Test of Immediate History*, Paris: Karthala.

Weber, Max (1963) "The scientist and politics", *UGE*, 10(18) pp. 76 and 184, quoted in François Borella (1990) *Critique of political knowledge*, Paris: PUF, pp. 90–91.

Willame, Jean-Claude (1997) *Banyarwanda and Banyamulenge: Ethnic Violence and Identity Management in Kivu*, Brussels and Paris: African Institute/ L'Harmattant.

——— (1972) *Patrimonialism and Political Change in the Congo*, Stanford CA: Stanford University Press.

7

Accessing the child's voice: Methods used in South Africa

Jacqui Gallinetti

The twentieth century has seen a proliferation of ethnic conflicts on various continents – Europe, Africa, and in the East. In addition to the obvious violent consequences of such conflict, such as mass executions and the rape and torture of innocent victims, the effects of community displacement, family disintegration, and poverty on peoples subjected to ethnic conflict have far-reaching consequences that go beyond the immediate hostilities.

Héraud (1979: 26) has defined "ethnic" as delineating a group of people sharing the same combination of characteristics concerning language, religion and/or cultural tradition. Further to this, Kruitenbrouwer (1999) describes ethnic conflict as being collective action, non-violent or violent, of an ethnic group against a dominant ethnic group in a state where the dominant group often controls the state authorities. It is also where the state, acting on behalf of the dominant ethnic group, takes violent or non-violent action to suppress manifestations of ethnic collective action by a non-dominant ethnic group. The latter is an example of the situation in South Africa during the years of apartheid rule.

There are many aspects to ethnic conflicts that make them so necessary to research. As stated already, these types of conflicts have far-reaching consequences that can be both internal and external. The internal consequences often are manifested in day-to-day life within the area that the conflict spans – for example, the loss of homes, family members, social disintegration, and deprivation of basic human rights. The external consequences relate to the internationalization of the ethnic conflict where other states become involved in the conflict, and this in turn can lead to international power struggles that threaten world stability (Premdas, 1991: 10). Recent examples of this are the Arab–Israeli conflict as well as the Balkan conflicts that spanned the 1990s. The South African situation under the apartheid years has been identified by Premdas as an example of an armed conflict that had the potential to threaten global security because of the country's strategic location and abundance of mineral resources (ibid.: 9).

This chapter will concentrate on aspects of ethnic conflicts that relate to the internal consequences and, particularly, the consequences for children. It will look at the need to access the child's voice in order to obtain a holistic approach to understanding the consequences of ethnic conflict. By including the child's opinions in this type of research, a more comprehensive picture can emerge so that appropriate policy decisions can be made in order to combat and heal the effects of ethnic conflict.

The age-old adage – a child should be seen and not heard – indicates the position accorded to children in the past. They have been seen as objects not worthy of expressing a meaningful opinion, and historically their views have not been taken account of or even sought out. However, with the advent of the seminal human rights document on children's rights – the United Nations Convention on the Rights of the Child (UNCRC) – this perception of the value of children's voices has, theoretically, been obliterated.

The difficulty in discussing the child's right to be heard in the context of the UNCRC and ethnic conflict is what Kruitenbrouwer (1999: 9) terms the "intellectual gap between anthropology and international law". Anthropology and international law view human rights as the formal unity of humanity sanctioned by international treaties and upheld by the international community against a Western backdrop of natural law. On the other hand, anthropology looks to the informal yet fundamental division of humanity in different ethnic or national cultures and their collectivist nature, which is mostly prevalent among non-Western peoples. However, as all countries in the world have ratified the UNCRC – with the exception of Somalia and the United States of America – I will note the dichotomy, but nevertheless proceed to discuss the child's right to be heard as set out in the document.

Article 12 of the UNCRC constitutes one of the general principles and aims of the Convention – namely, to ensure children's participation. According to the document, the child is no longer seen as an object or possession, but as a person capable of forming views that need to be taken into account in decisions affecting his or her life.

The child's voice and the Convention on the Rights of Children

Article 12 of the UNCRC has introduced a comprehensive provision standardizing the child's right to express views and be heard. It states as follows:

12.1 State Parties shall assure to the child who is capable of forming his or her own views the right to express those views freely in all matters affecting the child, the views of the child being given due weight in accordance with the age and maturity of the child.

12.2 For this purpose, the child shall in particular be provided the opportunity to be heard in any judicial and administrative proceedings affecting the child, either directly, or through a representative or an appropriate body, in a manner consistent with the procedural rules of national law. (UNCRC, Art. 12.1, 12.2)

Article 12(1) is of a far more general application than Article 12(2), which focuses on the right of the child to be heard, in person or duly represented, in specific proceedings affecting himself or herself. Article 12(1) allows the child a free reign to participate in all levels of decision-making, both public and private. This can range from participation in drafting of legislation and policy-making to family decisions.

Interpreting Article 12

As stated above, Article 12 has both a general aspect and a more specific application of the right to be heard. This encompasses a number of concepts – namely, participation, freedom of expression, and the right to be heard. These afford children a mechanism to make their voices heard in matters affecting their lives.

Interestingly, the right to hold an opinion (as opposed to express an opinion) as contained in the International Covenant on Civil and Political Rights is not found in the UNCRC. This is not a crucial failing on the part of the drafters but does tend to minimize the importance of a child's ability to formulate opinions (Van Bueren, 1995: 136). Its exclusion from the Convention is also illogical as the right to hold an opinion is a precondition to the right to freedom of expression. Nevertheless, the UNCRC focuses on expressing the opinion rather than the opinion itself.

Within the Convention, there is a strong focus on the child as an individual. This can be seen in the right of the child to his or her identity, nationality, name, and family relations (Article 8), the right of the child to freedom of expression (Article 13), the right of the child to freedom of thought, conscience, and religion (Article 14), and the right of the child to freedom of association (Article 15). Article 12 also supports the notion of the child as an individual as it provides the right to the child to express his or her views and opinions and thereby his or her individuality. However, a necessary corollary to this is the requirement that the child is then listened to when expressing the opinion or exercising the right to be heard. It can be argued that by placing an obligation on states, in Article 4, to undertake all measures to ensure the implementation of the rights in the UNCRC this is achieved. However, the question is raised whether this is sufficient. Van Bueren argues that, in addition, there needs to be changes in the culture of listening (2000: 203). She states:

The Convention on the Rights of the Child requires the State and therefore society, to regard children as evolving autonomous individuals. This implies walking the journey with the child's eyes. Adults have to be willing to relinquish some of their own power before a new culture of listening seriously to children can develop (Van Bueren, 2000: 205).

Therefore, the issue extends beyond the mere legal obligation placed on member states by Article 4 of the UNCRC. Adults traditionally have decided matters affecting children according to their own means of reasoning and their own perceptions of what is in the best interests of children. A change must now occur that necessarily entails actively listening to the voices of children and giving appropriate weight to the opinions and views expressed by them by recognizing that children have the capacity to reason and rationalize the issues at hand, whatever they may be (Van Bueren, 2000: 206).

Listening and heeding views is especially the case when dealing with ethnic conflict. Hostilities, whether violent or non-violent, have significant impact on children. The study undertaken in Northern Ireland by Marie Smyth (1998) is illustrative of this. She notes that conflict is experienced by children in the context of the effect thereof on the assets, resources, impediments, and handicaps of the child in his or her wider social context (ibid.: 15). The study illustrates how the Troubles have affected, *inter alia*, children's educational performance (ibid.: 19), employment (ibid.: 20), and family situation (ibid.: 26). Such a comprehensive study is a valuable tool for government, NGOs, and INGOs in trying to establish policy and solutions for the hostilities and in simply setting in place mechanisms to deal with the consequences of the situation. The children have had an opportunity to have a say – now they should be listened to.

In order for this change in the culture of listening to occur, there has to be a clear understanding of the import and implications of the contents of Article 12. The nature of the Article is such that it is drafted with sufficient detail to be implementable and self-executing (of direct application) (Lücker-Babel, 1995: 395). The UNCRC requires states to respect the rights contained therein (Article 2) and take appropriate measures to ensure this is achieved (Article 4). Therefore, the Convention has adopted a flexible approach and left the matter to member states to implement its provisions in their national laws. The extent to which national courts and institutions can play a role in this depends on whether certain provisions of the Convention are of direct application as well as the status of the Convention in national law.

In addition and at the outset, it is also important to note that the rights of the child to express his or her views and to be heard are not unrestricted. They are subject to the important provisos that children who are capable of forming views should be heard and their views be given due weight according to their age and maturity.

Interpretation of Article 12(1)

State parties are obliged to "assure" to the child the right to express his or her views. This ensures that states do not hold children directly accountable in the decision-making process and force them to make a decision or express their opinion; it merely obliges states to afford children the opportunity to be heard and participate by allowing them access to the decision-making process (Van Bueren, 1995: 137). This ensures the child the freedom to choose whether or not to actually participate in any process. This is an important consideration when the child may have witnessed or experienced atrocities accompanying violence.

Article 12(1) has very broad application in that it refers to the child expressing his or her views in "all matters affecting the child". Thus, the scope of the child's participation is not limited to a closed list of instances as was proposed in the drafting process of this Article (Detrick, 1992: 215). The implication is that the state is now obliged to assure the child the opportunity to express his or her views in relation to public and private sphere issues and in relation to the latter, it appears the child has a right to participate actively in the historically closed arena of family decision-making (Van Bueren, 1995: 137). This wording also ensures the child's ability to participate in matters that extend beyond the scope of the Convention itself (Lücker-Babel, 1995: 395).

By using the word "child" in Article 12 as opposed to the word "children", it appears the drafters have attempted to limit the application of the Article to situations that directly affect a particular individual child (ibid.: 396). However, this does not mean to say that a particular child may not participate in a decision-making process that affects him or her but that which at the same time affects children generally. An example of this is the process of consulting with children around law reform of legislation directly affecting them, such as welfare or childcare laws. Children who are a part of the child-care system obviously would have a direct interest in the law reform, but their participation would necessarily have the effect of a wider application for all children.

The inclusion of the term "freely" is of great importance. It re-inforces the fact that states are not obliging the child to participate in the decision-making process – only assuring them the right to. It requires the child's participation not only to be voluntary but also that the views and opinions expressed are indeed the child's own. This is of particular relevance when dealing with a situation where the child is involved in a family decision or a decision involving his or her parents, as the pos-sibilities for direct and indirect influence over the child are vast. This also places a duty on the authority or decision-maker to ensure that the child has not been subject to coercion or duress in participating, that the voice heard is indeed that of the child's and that the opinion or view expressed has been informed by all the available information (ibid.: 398). It is obvious that if the child has formed an opinion without the benefit of accurate and complete information, then the view expressed is lacking in weight.

Limitations to the rights contained in Article 12

The words "For this purpose" relate Article 12(2) directly back to the content of Article 12(1). This is of particular significance when looking at the restrictions of the right of the child to express his or her views and be heard as the restrictions apply to both sub-articles and have impli-cations for decision-makers, researchers and child representatives in applying Article 12.

There are two restrictions in question, namely, the rights in Article 12 are only extended to children who are capable of forming their own views and those views are only given due weight according to the age and maturity of the child in question. Lücker-Babel states that the capacity of a child to form his or her own views does not mean that the child must be fully developed to do so, as the second limitation then applies – requiring a decision-making body only to give weight to those views in accordance with the age and maturity of the child (1995: 397). She goes on to reason that the first step is to determine whether the child is in a position to form a view on an issue in question, but not on the whole range of issues in a particular case (1995: 397). Following this reasoning even an *infans* can participate where his or her feelings are interpreted by an appropriate expert (ibid.: 397) and then those feelings are given due weight according to his or her age and maturity.

By making use of the requirement that a child need only be capable of forming his or her own views, the UNCRC is allowing a greater number of children to participate in decisions, as the child's capacity varies according to his or her individual development and his or her capacity to understand the nature of and events in question is not necessarily dependant on his or her age (Lücker-Babel, 1995: 397). Once it has been determined whether a child has the capacity to form an opinion, the inquiry shifts to the weight to be given to that opinion. The two determining factors are the age (an objective determinant) and maturity (a subjective determinant) of the child (ibid.: 399). These two factors are of equal value (Van Bueren, 1995: 136). It is argued that the more serious the consequences of the decision are, the more the child's opinion needs to be considered with regard to the nature of the problem and the degree of interest it represents to the child (Lücker-Babel, 1995: 399). Again, advocating a change in the culture of listening, Van Bueren states, in relation to these two tests:

For children truly to be heard the listener has to understand the language of the child in order to assess whether, in accordance with the Convention, the child is capable of expressing views. The sole test is that of capability, not of age or maturity (2000: 206).

Implementing Article 12(1)

While Article 12(2) focuses on the child's right to be heard in particular proceedings that are of an official nature, Article 12(1) focuses on the child expressing his or her views as an individual generally in matters affecting him or her in particular, as opposed to matters affecting children as a whole.

In its *Guidelines for Periodic Reports*, the Committee on the Rights of the Child requires that the reporting country should provide information on legislative and other measures taken to ensure the right of the child to express views on all matters affecting him or her, which include family life, school life, the administration of juvenile justice, placement and life in institutional and other forms of care, and in asylum-seeking procedures (Hodgkin and Newell, 1998: 146). It is clear, however, that the scope of the instances in which a child can become involved in expressing his or her views is vast and expansive. Ethnic conflict – a situation that affects the lives of all peoples subjected thereto – is a prime example of a situation that cries out for consultation with children. Such consultation is particularly pertinent given the increasing numbers of child-headed households that emerge as a consequence of intense violence or genocide, or when children in displaced families become separated from their parents in seeking asylum and must fend for themselves.

Hodgkin and Newell list a number of instances where children have been given opportunities to participate and express their views in government and policy-making (1998: 154–6). For example, Costa Rica initiated children's elections, in which children were given the opportunity to express their views on a range of issues that they felt were important and needed immediate attention; the government then took steps to ensure that these views were taken into account in policy-making decisions. Working with children through schools, Slovenia undertook a consultation process in which the children could express their views on matters of concern to them. In addition, a structured system of consultation was undertaken, beginning with school parliaments, which then met at municipal level on an annual basis and this culminated in a Children's Parliament convened by the National Assembly at which children's deputies, municipal representatives, NGOs, and government ministers were represented.

Children's voices in South Africa

One of the most direct ways a child can have an impact on decisions affecting his or her life is by expressing his or her views in relation to child-specific law reform. In this respect, South Africa has undertaken two innovative initiatives in consulting with children. Since the advent of a constitutional democracy in 1994 and South Africa's ratification of the UNCRC in 1995, there has been a law reform process initiated in respect of juvenile justice and childcare laws. The South African Law Commission released its Report on Juvenile Justice together with a draft Child Justice Bill in July 2000. In 2002, the Commission reviewed the Child Care Act (Act 74 of 1983), with a comprehensive consultation with children and released its Children's Bill in December 2002.

The Project Committee on the Review of the Child Care Act commissioned a report on giving effect to Article 12 of the UNCRC from an NGO. The investigation, undertaken in 1999, was aimed at a review of the childcare legislation, together with the common law, customary law, and religious laws relating to children in South Africa (Community Law Centre, 1999: 3). The means undertaken to achieve this investigation involved a series of focus-group discussions with children ranging from 5 to 18 years of age who had direct experience with the Child Care Act (ibid.: 4). The consultation process included: a group session to introduce the children to children's rights, the law, and the role of government; a process whereby each child interviewed one or more of their peers to obtain a wider opinion; and a focus group to address the questions raised by the Law Commission (ibid.: 4–5). The children who were consulted included children in institutional care, children in foster or informal care, disabled children, street children, children who had experienced abuse, and children who had been involved in legal proceedings (ibid.: 6). By selecting these groups of children to participate in the consultations, Article 12 was given effect in that these children were expressing views on legislation directly affecting them.

One of the conclusions of the study was that the responses obtained from the groups were largely predictable; however it was stated that the consultations were nonetheless:

worthwhile in obtaining the opinions of children in an unpressurized, natural manner and, rather, than attempting to filter these responses through adult judgements about what is a profound contribution and what is not, these opinions should be seen as worthwhile for what they are (Community Law Centre, 1999: 62).

The Project Committee on Juvenile Justice of the South African Law Commission also consulted with children in the drafting of the Child Justice Bill, which aims to revolutionize the criminal justice system in South Africa as it pertains to children, to bring it in line with constitutional and international obligations. The aim of the study was to ask children for their views on various aspects of the draft Child Justice Bill released for public comment by the South African Law Commission in December 1998 (Children's Rights Project, 1998–99: 7). This consultation process differed from the one undertaken in relation to the Child Care Act in that it was more specific to issues relating to child justice, whereas the former was more general in its scope.

The children who were selected to participate included children in a diversion programme, children under the age of 12 and children over the age of 14 awaiting trial in a place of safety, children awaiting trial in prison, children serving a sentence in a reformatory and those serving a sentence in prison, and a group of scholars who had never been in trouble with the law (ibid.: 40). Methods of consultation included role-playing, small group discussions and individual written feedback, and children were asked to share their experiences of the present system of criminal justice and comment on the proposed changes (ibid.: 8).

It has been said that the consultation with children in the child justice sphere provides an excellent example of how public participation can strengthen policy and legislation and how the participation of children in the law-making process in South Africa has enriched the dialogue of making children's voices heard (de Villiers, 2001: 59–62).

As far as research methodology is concerned, these two studies have illustrated the need to be aware of the environment in which a particular child is situated when undertaking child participation research. This is of particular significance in conflict-ridden-societies where children may be traumatized by the effects of violence on their lives. South Africa is a large country and has very diverse communities. There are numerous factors that influence a child's situation, a key one of which is geography – where the child is situated. Children's experiences have been shown to be different depending on the area in which they live. There is a huge divide between children situated in urban areas and those situated in rural areas. In addition, the Western Cape has a particular problem with gangs – a phenomenon that is not prevalent elsewhere in the country. The Eastern Cape and the Northern Province are the most poverty-stricken provinces in South Africa and this has an important bearing on the resources available for children and what they have been exposed to, compared with children situated in other areas of South Africa.

These concerns echo the complexities noted by Liddell et al. (1994: 51–3) in discussing the complexities in understanding the cultural diversity of children in South Africa. They state that ethnicity in the South African context is questionable as a meaningful discriminatory construct as factors such as local ecology, subsistence modes, and patterns of social organization will have a bearing on this. Also noted is the fact that within individual cultures, rural–urban markers are used to make distinctions between groups as this gives rise to divisions based on socio-economic status, especially when dealing with differences in family life, household organization, and child behaviour. The authors warn that cultural descriptors such as ethnicity and urbanicity should be examined in a broader analytical framework and not in isolation, as it is only by examining these concepts in conjunction with one another that a better understanding of their effects on children's behaviour can be achieved. In addition, as far as methodology is concerned, when dealing with divergent cultures, it obviously is important that researchers who are conversant with the language and customs of the children should be used.

Another factor that emerged from the juvenile justice participation study was the difficulty in explaining the purpose of the study to children accused of committing crimes who were awaiting trial in prison. The study was purely voluntary; however, the researcher formed the impression that the children awaiting trial felt that if they did not participate this would somehow have an adverse affect on their case. It is very important to dispel this notion as the nature of child participation is based on the freedom of choice to participate; no child should feel pressured into taking part in this type of research. It is factors such as these that have to be borne in mind when undertaking a study to allow children to express their opinions in order for there to be accuracy and a valid understanding of the results of the research.

The South African experience and ethnic conflict

In discussing the policy of apartheid in South Africa, Professor Moosa, Head of Applied Psychology at the University of the Witwatersrand, stated that it "not only fosters conditions conducive to child abuse and neglect, but is in itself abusive" (quoted in Fourie, 1990: 106). Fourie notes that the civil unrest that occurred in the townships during the apartheid years subjected South African children to extensive trauma by them being witnesses to deaths, being subjected to indiscriminate arrest and constant harassment by the police and security forces, as well as ongoing discrimination (ibid.).

The apartheid laws enacted by the white ruling class and imposed on the "colored", "Asian" and "African" population (according to classifications used in the Population Registration Act of 1950) have created a situation whereby the oppressed, and in particular children who are among the most vulnerable of our society, are impoverished, poorly educated, and unemployed. In addition, family disintegration was, and remains, a predominant consequence of the poor economic situation that forces breadwinners to leave their homes in search of work in the cities, moving especially to seek work in the mines.

Dawes and Donald have noted that psychological research around the developmental issues affecting children in South Africa has been minimal (1994a: 6). They note too that children's responses to adverse circumstances are complex and that there is a lack of understanding of how they deal with such hardship. They pose the question of how best to study these children (1994: 9). This is the core question. Obviously for the psychology discipline there are norms relating to the undertaking of research. These norms however must necessarily now include adherence to the spirit of the UNCRC – namely, child participation. The standards and rationale behind Article 12 must be given due attention in consulting with and researching children. This necessarily involves assessing the child's capacity to express an opinion and must be focused on the voluntary nature of the child's participation. Again, although one is engaged with research, it must be conducted in a culture of listening in order to extract what is beneficial for the child, and not from the adult perspective of obtaining research data for compilation in a study. The importance of listening to the child and making the child feel that his or her contribution is important and will be taken into account should be of paramount consideration.

In researching the emotional consequences of political violence on children in South Africa, Dawes has identified certain problems influencing the quality of research and conclusions that can be drawn (1994: 179). First, is the loose term "political violence" as this can range from being detained without trial to witnessing the death of a parent. One has to identify the particular situation for the individual child and thus the specific effect of political violence on the child. Second, one cannot compare simplistically conflict situations from different countries with the situation in South Africa, which, as he notes, has been done in the past. Third, he indicates that the definition of "childhood" presents its own particular problems as different communities have differing notions of childhood. As mentioned already, in some war-torn zones, orphaned children are now heading households. It is very difficult, therefore, to proceed without a clear notion. The South African Law Commission released a discussion paper ("Review of the Child Care Act", Discussion Paper 103) in 2001 wherein they are attempting to define the notion of childhood. A subsequent substantial "Review of the Child Care Act" was released in December 2002. Finally, methodology presents difficulties surrounding appropriate sampling, controls, and follow-up studies. Dawes (1994) notes, as have other authors in this book, that it is problematic conducting research in conflict situations because of the attendant danger in entering conflict zones.

Further, as far as methodology in researching children's responses to violence is concerned, Dawes notes that most international research in this area is focused on the way in which negative life circumstances render children vulnerable to developmental problems (1994a: 184). This is termed the "life events approach". This approach looks at a number of factors affecting childhood development, including sensitizing and steeling effects, delayed effects, active and passive coping styles, and transitory events (ibid.: 186–7). With the exception of studies in passive and active coping styles, almost none of these factors have been researched to any great extent in South Africa.

Conclusion

It is clear that there is an international obligation to consult with children and, in South Africa, because of the ratification of the CRC, this also translates into a domestic obligation – likewise for all other countries who have ratified the Convention without qualifying the ratification in respect of Article 12. The duty is therefore there, when conducting ethnic research, to include the child's voice, and it is submitted that this is a fundamental and important part of any research in the area. Children are the most vulnerable and disenfranchised members of society, and inevitably it is they who are directly affected by ethnic conflict. If we are to find solutions and put plans into action to combat such conflict, children's opinions need to be taken into account. At the very least, policy towards ethnic conflict, whether it be international or national, should be framed with a child's perspective being one of the informing factors. Obviously how to access children within particular conflict situation needs to be informed by the peculiarities and features of that situation, but the underlying call is to include the child in all research in this area where it is appropriate to do so.

REFERENCES

Children's Rights Project (1998–99) *Report on Children's Rights: "They should listen to our side of the story"*, Cape Town: Community Law Centre, University of the Western Cape.

Community Law Centre (1999) *Report on workshops held to give effect to Article 12 of the United Nations Convention on the Rights of the Child (Children's Participation)*, Cape Town: University of the Western Cape.

De Villiers, Susan (2001) *A People's Government. The People's Voice*, Cape Town: The Parliamentary Support Programme.

Dawes, Andrew (1994) "The emotional impact of political violence", in Andrew Dawes and David Donald, eds., *Childhood and Adversity*, Cape Town: David Philip Publishers, pp. 177–199.

Dawes, Andrew and Donald, David (1994) "Understanding the psychological consequences of adversity", in Andrew Dawes and David Donald, eds., *Childhood and Adversity*, Cape Town: David Philip Publishers, pp. 1–27.

Detrick, Sharon (1992) *The UN Convention on the Rights of the Child*, Dordrecht: Kluwer.

Fourie, Enid (1990) "The UN Convention on the Rights of the Child and the crisis for children in South Africa: apartheid and detention", *Human Rights Quarterly* 12(106): 106–114.

Héraud, Guy (1979) *L Europe des ethnies*, 2nd edn., Paris: Presses d'Europe.

Hodgkin, Rachel and Newell, Peter (1998) *Implementation Handbook for the Convention on the Rights of the Child*, New York: UNICEF.

Kruitenbrouwer, Maarten (1999) "Ethnic conflicts and human rights: multidisciplinary and interdisciplinary perspectives", in Peter Baehr, Floribert Baudet, and Hans Werdmölder, eds., *Human Rights and Ethnic Conflicts*, Utrecht: Netherlands Institute of Human Rights SIM Special No. 24, pp. 7–24.

Liddell, Christine, Kvalsvig, Jane, Shabalala, Agnes, and Qotyana, Pumla (1994) "Defining the cultural context of children's everyday experiences in the year before school", in Andrew Dawes and David Donald, eds., *Childhood and Adversity*, Cape Town: David Philip Publishers, pp. 51–65.

Lücker-Babel, M. (1995) "The Rights of the Child to Express Views and be Heard: An Attempt to Interpret Article 12 of the UN Convention on the Rights of the Child", *The International Journal of Children's Rights* 3(3–4): 391–404.

Premdas, Ralph R. (1991) "The internationalisation of ethnic conflict: some theoretical explorations", in Kingsley M. De Silva and Ronald James May, eds., *Internationalization of Armed Conflict*, London: Pinter, pp. 10–25.

Smyth, Marie (1998) *Half the Battle: Understanding the Effects of the "Troubles" on Children and Young People in Northern Ireland*, Derry/Londonderry: INCORE.

Van Bueren, Geraldine (1995) *The International Law on the Rights of the Child*, Dordrecht/London: Martinus Nijhoff.

———— (2000) "The United Nations Convention on the Rights of the Child: an evolutionary revolution", in Catherina Johanna Davel, ed., *An Introduction to Child Law in South Africa*, Cape Town: Juta Law, pp. 202–213.

8

Certainty, subjectivity, and truth: Reflections on the ethics of wartime research in Angola

J. Zoë Wilson

"A thousand years ago, we thought the world was a bowl", he said. "Five hundred years ago we knew it was a globe. Today we know it is flat and round and carried through space on the back of a turtle." He turned and gave the high priest another smile. "Don't you wonder what shape it will turn out to be tomorrow"? (Terry Pratchett, *The Truth*)

The United Nations and its non-governmental organization (NGO) partners are often the key conduits for international researchers endeavouring to carry out research in a conflict zone. Based on time-bound research in Angola (2001), this chapter highlights some of the theoretical, practical, ethical, and political dimensions involved with doing short-term, time-bound research through UN diplomatic and humanitarian channels.

The chapter proceeds in four subsequent parts. First, I offer a brief description of the research project to which the methodological reflections below pertain. Second, I discuss the theoretical and ethical issues that informed the emancipatory thrust of the project. Specifically, I argue that if, indeed, theory and methodology is always for someone for some purpose (Cox, 1981), then determining one's approach means more than deciding how to evaluate truth claims embedded in prior research in order to determine how to employ new field research towards representing the overall body of facts more accurately. It means wading into the contested terrain and politics of truth production. Third, I discuss how and why I relied on the UN as a conduit for my research. I address practical questions such as accessing the UN and funding, what to expect, personal security, mobility, independence/accompaniment, translators, the operational benefits and drawbacks of working through the UN machinery and, ultimately, within UN narrativized spaces – themselves embedded in UN norms and Security Council mandates. Finally, I discuss some of the specific ethical questions that I encountered when devising my interview strategy, and why ultimately I decided to interview only international staff and government officials, except in specific circumstances.

Introduction to the research project

Luanda is the city of splendid squalor. A breathtakingly beautiful landscape tethered to a colonial artefact in the final stages of decay, where absolute vulnerability stands shoulder to shoulder with frontier prosperity, and existential uncertainty stands ready for abrupt recombination of mass and void. Angolans are a people on a precipice, their hope and dreams a sacrifice on the altar of history.

It is a history of brutal and pernicious colonialism, ending only after a fierce struggle for independence waged by desperate and disparate guerrillas, turned freedom fighters, when the brutal dictatorship of Salazar in Portugal finally crumbled under revolution in 1974. But independence was short lived. No sooner was independence negotiated, than Apartheid South Africa rolled into the South, hoping to quash the Namibian (then South West African) freedom fighters, SAWPO (South West Africa People's Organization), operating out of Southern Angola. With the aid of UNITA (*Uniao Nacional para a Independencia Total de Angola*) (and covert assistance from the United States and its client state Zaire), the South African Defence Force (SADF) continued to wage war in Angola, advancing year by year. Along the way, SADF/UNITA met with steadfast resistance from the MPLA (*Movimento Popular de Libertaçao de Angola*), aided by the Cubans (and enormous international debts), and in 1987 a decisive battle was waged at Cuito Cuanaval.

The defeat of the South Africans is largely interpreted as the end of South African expansionism. Within two years, Namibia would be the last African country to achieve independence, through the peacekeeping operation (PKO) UNTAG (United Nations Transitions Assistance Group). It was not long before the UN turned its attention to Angola. By 1992 it had negotiated a settlement between UNITA and the MPLA and scheduled elections. During what was the cheapest PKO in history, few played by the "rules", with UNITA in particular using the PKO as a cover for re-armament. In the aftermath of a questionable election (Heywood, 2000), war resumed. UNITA, in particular, was strategically prepared for total military onslaught, and more civilians died than in the entire history of the war up until that point.

During successive peace talks and PKOs, the MPLA also re-armed and stepped up its campaign to counter-balance UNITA. Recently, however, the MPLA has lost patience with the UN, and decided victory over UNITA is the only option; the legacy of covert international assistance, the failure of the PKOs to prevent UNITA from re-arming during the peace processes, unreasonable demands for transparency and market reform, and the failure of the international sanctions regime against conflict diamonds, all combined to convince the MPLA that the UN presence was a duplicitous one that did more harm than good.

In order to defeat UNITA and maintain control over the state, however, the MPLA has adopted "depopulation" campaigns designed to purge the countryside of UNITA supporters. Today, millions of people are internally displaced, crowded into under-resourced internally displaced persons (IDP) camps hosted by the UN and its NGO partners. Sickness and malnutrition are endemic. Almost half the population of Angola has fled to Luanda, a city built for 200,000, now home to 4–5 million, most of whom live in squalid and overcrowded barrios. But, this is a process that started before independence as tribal peoples fled forced labour and draconian hut taxes. "In this light", Jeremy Harding observed (1993: 72):

Luanda had seemed an impressive place. Its very degeneration was heroic, and even its poverty. So was the perversity of the system, the arrogance of the party, the ruthless unavailability of ministers and officials. It was all the monolithic offspring of necessity. Pretoria had drubbed Mozambique, squeezed Namibia, and punished its own opposition, Angola had stood its ground. It had also paid dearly, in lives and in oil revenues, for supporting the ANC against Apartheid and SAWPO against the occupation of Namibia.

But is modern Angola simply the legacy of the past? Is peace as simple as moving on in a more enlightened age? If so, why has peace been so elusive? Do, as some analysts suggest, post-Cold War narrations of peace, progress, and development in the form of peacekeeping, democratization, and "unleashed markets" simply hold Angola true to the perverse course of socio-cultural disintegration and political authoritarianism, instigated by the Portuguese, hastened by the advent of international resource chains (Davidson, 1975; Reno, 1998), and affirmed and reaffirmed by successive "development" failures, whose catastrophic results are paradoxically reinterpreted as the justification for the West's entitlement to "develop and democratize the South in its own image" (Abrahamsen, 2000: xi)? Or, have African leaders become so avaricious that they ferment war rather than expend the most meagre of state wealth on the nation-building project (Hodges, 2001)?

Answering these questions is a complex proposition, but the first steps bring us directly to the doorstep of complex peacekeeping operations, comprising peacemaking (diplomacy), peacekeeping (troop deployment), and peace-building (post-conflict reconstruction). There have, in fact, been two peacemaking missions, four peacekeeping missions, and an ongoing peace-building mission since 1989. These PKOs comprise the bulk of the multilateral engagement (as opposed to bi-lateral and multi-national trade) with Angola, and bear little resemblance to their inter-state ancestors. Rather, they seek to address the multidimensional aspects of peace-brokering, peace-enforcement, peace-maintenance, and peace-building. These expanded strategies of peace attempt to integrate everything from macro-economic restructuring to grassroots human-rights awareness. Recently, we have seen them include military presence, humanitarian assistance, human-rights advocacy, elections, macro-economic restructuring, political institution-building, constructive engagement, and the like. Mark Duffield (2001: 13) has described these multidimensional peace operations as "the strategic complexes of liberal peace", and points to "emerging relations between governments, NGOs, militaries, and the business sector" as their hallmark.

In reality, action is complex, layered and uncoordinated, but:

the idea of *liberal peace* ... combines and conflates "liberal" (as in contemporary liberal economic and political tenants) with "peace" (the present policy predilec-tion toward conflict resolution and societal reconstruction). It reflects the existing consensus that conflict in the South is best approached through a number of connected, ameliorative, harmonizing and, especially, transformational measures. While this can include the provision of immediate relief and rehabilitation assis-tance, liberal peace embodies a new political humanitarianism that lays emphasis on such things as conflict resolution and prevention, reconstructing social net-works, strengthening civil and representative institutions, promoting the rule of law and security sector reform in the context of a functioning market economy. In many respects while contested and far from assured, liberal peace reflects a radical development agenda of social transformation (Duffield 2001: 13).

This research project evaluates the conflict resolution and emancipa-tory potential of the PKO/Angola nexus by synthesizing local, national, and international levels of analysis in order to contribute to the debates about peace, but, perhaps more importantly, to further freedom, justice, and self-determination for the people who live in the former Portuguese colonial state of Angola. It does so in light of its history, structures of global governance, liberal globalism, emerging structures of external governance, dense networks of interest that support transnational com-modity chains, regionalism, and the corresponding trends in minimal sovereignty and low-intensity democracy.

Theory and ethics

Contemporary multilateral discourse about war and peace (and peace-keeping) in Africa centres on the scale of humanitarian catastrophe that results from the systemic targeting of civilian populations. Affronted by the suffering of the innocents, the UN has proclaimed its allegiance to "peace" and a commitment to "confront the lingering forces of war and violence, with the ability and determination to defeat them" (United Nations, 2000: viii). Towards this end, the UN had proclaimed that impartiality will no longer mean impartiality in terms of political neutrality, but rather "impartiality for the United Nations operations must ... mean adherence to the principles of the Charter" in order to avoid "complicity with evil" (2000: ix).

Critical scholars of the UN Charter and international law (Brown, 1999; Charlesworth, 1993; Grovogui, 1996) argue, however, that there is nothing impartial about the UN Charter. The nuances of these arguments aside, it is worth noting that the Charter represents a community of states, and inherently is conservative, vowing to defend existing sovereignties in the interest of international peace and security. The problem with this model, however, was that:

In the world that was taking shape in the 1950s, the colonial structure of the late 1940s was the last thing that the majority of states wanted to preserve. For the newly created nations – and even more, those still aspiring to nationhood – the world was dynamic rather than static. Peace was to be sought not in the maintenance of order, but in the securing of justice. It was something to be achieved, if necessary fought for, rather than preserved (Howard in Adibe, 1998: 110).

This raises some important questions about the complexities and contradictions between concerns about civilians and defending sovereignties. Especially given that "the number of battle deaths for all international and civil wars in this century is 30 million and seven million respectively; the total number of civilians killed by governments (excluding war) is 170 million" (Thakur, 1999: 53). In this context, the UN assumption that it is necessary to reconstitute the state and consolidate its power to maintain order may be the first assumption that the researcher of peace and conflict should discard (Adibe, 1998: 109).

It is equally problematic to assume that an end to the war, at any cost, is the fundamental desire of people in conflict zones – and here I mean specifically liberal iterations of political and market reform characterized by successive deepening of the structures of external governance. War, as noted by Clausewitz (1976), is politics by other means. It is as much heinous violence as it is a historical process that reconfigures power relations in the absence of the means to resolve deep conflict non-violently (Chingono, unpublished).

The first and obvious point is that the conflicting parties are likely, at least in their own estimation to be fighting for a good reason: conflicts which from the outside appear "irrational" and meaninglessly destructive will almost invariably seem to those engaged in them to be very important indeed, endowed with a "rationale" for which they are prepared to risk their lives (Clapham, 1998: 305).

It is crucial, then, that researchers question their underlying assumptions – and where they come from – especially those that depoliticize the population, rendering them into "victims", "passengers", or "hostages", with no stake or interest in the order that emerges out of the conflict. As Nigerian writer and Nobel Laureate Wole Soyinka says, in his customary caustic style:

We are sometimes assailed by voices that have grown so insolently patronizing as to declare that Africans do not really care who governs them or how, as long as they are guaranteed freedom from diseases, shelter, and three square meals a day ... I do not propose to give one more second to such racial slurs, least of all when they are given voice from our own kith and kin in positions of, or slurping from the bloodied trough of, power (in Chabal, 1997: 10).

Confronting these kinds of assumptions was a central challenge when preparing a research agenda for Angola as a significant branch of the most recent literature tends to depict Angola as a resource cash cow embroiled in an elite war with few if any social, political, or ethnic foundations (Hodges, 2001). Counterviews exist (Malaquias, 2000). It was equally challenging to confront a humanitarian catastrophe of surreal proportion, which, unfortunately, is undisputed – and not think that the violence must end, by any means. But researchers must be wary of throwing their weight behind the shortest route to non-violence, particularly in the case of Africa where international strategies often reiterate rather than transform hierarchical structures of wealth, privilege, incentive, and exclusion (local and global), and the modalities of systemic violence that give birth to predators, rebels, "sobels", and freedom fighters.

Thus, "different analyses of what factors caused the [Angolan] conflict, and what factors keep it going reflect different preferences for the outcome and imply distinct prescriptions for peace" (Minter, 1994: 57). Going to the literature, in the first instance, reveals discrepancies and disjunctures between experts that speak to nuance, complexity, depth and multi-dimensionality. One also is confronted with endless silences and unknowable details, historical discontinuities, truncations, and contemporary disjunctures between rival theories bounded by disciplinary fences. Delineating the breadth of information about Angola and PKOs, therefore, meant beginning with an attempt to understand the contested terrain of truth, itself littered with theories, methodologies, assumptions, and concealed perspectives – and most saliently, a cast of endless ghosts, forgotten corpses strewn over the eschatological battlefields (Christianity/animism, white/black, civilized/savage) of long-ago dethroned beliefs, themselves rooted in interests and genealogies replete with accidents, surprises, miscalculations, and deviations.

That is, "reality is not unitary but differs according to where one stands" (Marks, 2000: 17). Cox applies this same sentiment to theory by arguing that there is no view from nowhere, and that theory, while it performs the necessary task of providing guidelines for data selection, filtering, and digestion in a world of infinite facts, "is always for someone for some purpose" (1981: 131). Thus, theoretical lenses, explicit or silent, at once help us to select from an infinite number of phenomena, to draw correlations, and to make sense of our world, but these lenses also shape what is perceived as relevant, important, mentionable, or even thinkable. To some extent, these lenses shape the social world. This raises important red flags for the researcher who is thinking about making a quest for truth.

Truth isn't outside power or lacking in power ... truth isn't the reward of free spirits, the child of protracted solitude, nor the privilege of those who have succeeded in liberating themselves. Truth is a thing of this world: it is produced only by virtue of multiple forms of constraint [structured social processes]. And it induces regular effects of power (Foucault in Marks, 2000: 133).

Thus, at the outset, I felt it was crucial to approach an understanding of Angola, not through traditional lenses, but as an unbounded physically, socially and intellectually contested terrain, mediated, and rendered only partially intelligible through complex, layered, and nested narratives, policed by silences, unknowable factors, and mystified by disjunctures between contemporary rival theories – *all stretched around the parameters of power.*

Hence, while most theories attempt to construct an image of Angola upon which the "international community" can act, some had much more power to enact the Angola – and its place in the international system – which they claimed to merely describe. Thus some regimes and institutions have the structural capacity to represent subjective knowledge as objective truth. This itself is power. A central referent for the research project therefore was that truth, particularly in the social sciences (about human nature, the human condition, and human potential), varies according to where one stands. Truth and power stand in dialectical relation where access to the production of truth is controlled by the structures of power, and these structures reproduce themselves through controlling access to truth – and excluding dissenting of *other* voices.

The argument is not, of course, that there are no material facts, but rather that social facts – those that exist because we believe in them, such as money, states, or Valentine's day (Ruggie, 1998) – represent the sometimes purposive, often accidental, culmination of selectively woven facts, truths, half-truths, untruths, and lies that are stretched around the parameters of the power they constitute. This is, as constructivists argue, the structure of what we *know* about the social world and the means through which that world is structured is contested. However, trading on the reflexivity of knowledge, constructivists believe that institutions can be reordered. This is only possible, however, through the disruption of existing mechanisms for the production and reproduction of truth – that is, the disassociation of structures of power from regimes of truth. For, if regimes of truth and structures of power stand together, will they also not fall together (Marks, 2000)?

Adopting subjectivity and the social construction of the social universe as a methodological referent point meant wading into the contested terrain of truth, and tempering my research agenda with the knowledge that a project designed to supplant present truths or falsehoods with new truths or falsehoods and challenge systems of truth and regimes of power with reinterpreted versions of themselves, was unethical. If I was made suspicious by many of the claims of those who professed to know what the Angolan people wanted, or what kind of conflict resolution or future development they needed, how could I, instead, embark on a project where I attributed that privileged mantle to myself? Furthermore, could I ignore the weight of history, colonialism, slavery, racism, each successive failed development decade (Bodely, 1994: 371) and with those events the awareness that some of "the most important problems [in the world today] derive from the practice of social science itself" (Delanty, 1997: 137)? Could I also ignore the dense network of national and international interests that not only construct knowledge about Angola and its people, but also benefit from the kinds of policy action and inaction entailed by the knowledge they create and disseminate? Did I, alone, think I could stand outside the epistemological anchors to which I am tethered and see and write from nowhere?

In response to the literature review and theory-building process, the research project's central referent became the dialectic of truth and power that PKOs supported, and its objective understanding of whether and where it empowered the people of Angola to mediate the trajectory of their own future non-violently,[1] and whether and where they entrenched or enacted "power over" the people of Angola, attempting to establish a "natural order of things" they have not chosen for themselves. Thus, my rationale for the project was the desire to participate in the deepening of deliberative political spaces and the disruption of "the political, economic, institutional regimes of the production of truth" where those are fundamentally exclusive, and, conversely, ultimately engage with "the possibility of constituting a new politics of truth" (Foucault in Marks, 2000: 134). This objective also contained a field component.

Introduction to field research

In April 2001, I spent a month in Angola, split between Luanda and the northern province of Uige. The research was tightly time-bound, and for various reasons could not be extended. I decided to keep my expectations, my plan, and my interview strategy simple, qualitative, and open-ended, expecting that flexibility and contingency would have to be my main assets in wartime research (Chingono, unpublished); thus, my approach was more journalistic than scientific. Despite my desire to keep it simple, however, adopting subjectivity and the social construction of the social universe as a methodological referent point meant making some important ethical decisions upfront, tempering my research agenda with the knowledge that a project designed to supplant present truths or falsehoods with new truths or falsehoods and challenge systems of truth and regimes of power with reinterpreted versions of themselves, was unethical. As would be, given my limited timeframe, any attempt to speak for or interpret the voice of Angolan people is unwarranted. If I was made suspicious by many of the claims of those who professed to know what the Angolan people wanted, or what kind of conflict resolution or future development they needed, how could I, instead, embark on a project where I attributed that privileged mantle to myself? Did I really think I could stand outside the western epistemological attachments to which I am tied? In the following two sections, I expand further on the implications of this stance.

In essence, I focused on gathering information on two basic questions: first, what was the *flavour* of power embedded in the Angola/PKO nexus and what kind of subjects did it seek to create (for example, empowered or dominated, or was it liberal and open-ended?); and second, what opportunities did the nexus hold for (even embryonic) steps toward the creation of domestic structures for self-determination? These are important and perplexing questions as David Sogge (2000: 6) remarks, noting that while few efforts have been made to date to involve civil society in agenda-setting in Angola, elsewhere "these are occasions created from the top down, and carry all the dangers of the hollow choiceless, 'low intensity' democracy that is an emerging hallmark of globalized governance in Africa today". In order to answer these questions, I examined the body of unpublished project data at the United Nations High Commission for Refugees (UNHCR) office in Luanda, attended interagency meetings, where representatives of all the UN offices met to discuss lessons learned and the trajectory of the entire mission, and conducted 18 interviews with government, military, NGO and UN staff in the provincial capital of Uige, as well as at site surveys, resulting in a comprehensive if limited microcosmic test case.

Logistics and working through the UN

Working through the UN was essential, both from the standpoint of logistics and personal security. In order to engage with the UN, I applied for an internship with the UNHCR in Angola, and was accepted. This would provide me with a letter of invitation to present to the Angolan visa office, with reception at the airport, a base out of which to work, and a network through which to find a place to live. UN internships are an excellent option because they are designed for student researchers and are expected to contribute to a research project. They are, however, unpaid, so funding must be secured elsewhere. This was a key factor because Luanda is an expensive city. After being accepted at UNHCR in Luanda, I put together a number of proposals for special funding, and was fortunate that the Canadian Department of National Defence was willing to fund this portion of my research.

While I had prepared a rough research agenda (expecting the unexpected), much of what ultimately transpired in Angola was the result of contingency. It worked in my favour that all the UN offices had been in the process of contraction since the MPLA had rejected further military presence. I was able to rent a reasonably priced and secure apartment (US$700/m) from an absent roving field officer, and usually was able to find or organize transportation, so few days were wasted. That said, I was still unprepared for the restrictions on movement in Luanda itself. Having travelled fairly extensively in Africa, I assumed that I would be able to move about freely in the long-held MPLA stronghold of Luanda. However, the intense overcrowding and relative deprivation made this an extremely risky prospect. There, I was entirely dependent on UN drivers for transportation.

The most significant unanticipated opportunity, was the recent transfer of their protection staff (human rights), my knowledge of the issue, and therefore easy deployment in that area, which led to me being sent up to the province of Uige to conduct and evaluate the UNHCR operation and the Human Rights Committee project. If I had not been working with the UN, research outside of Luanda would have been close to impossible. Road transportation between Luanda and other provincial capitals is impossible due to rebel activity, and the only passenger planes that fly regularly are World Food Programme (WFP) flights, and space is extremely limited.

Additionally, given my research topic, interview strategy, and time constraints, affiliation with the UN provided access to officials, meetings, documents, communication network, transportation, and translation. Furthermore, engaging with support staff offered important, if rare, opportunities to engage with savvy but locally embedded people who could provide important insights on trends and events.

The main area of concern that arose from working with the UN, particularly in Luanda, was the breadth and depth of the UN space I inhabited with its complex layers of different narratives. It became apparent that Angola, and Luanda in particular, is a series of highly stratified and somewhat unrelated worlds. Within the core, or internationalized space, there is also a UN culture from which it was difficult to stand apart. There were (contested) narratives that were immediately conspicuous. For example, the UN's operational mechanisms were uniformly unself-reflective (although I would not say the same for individual staff members), and this produced and reproduced discourses that privileged the appropriateness of the UN response and the legitimacy of its presence. Dennis Jett (1999: 2) in his study *Why Peacekeeping Fails?* commented on this tendency:

[A]fter the expenditure of $1.5 billion, a decade of effort, and the lives of over 60 peacekeepers, the UN Security Council officially recognised what it could not longer ignore [that the MPLA wanted them out]. It approved a resolution instructing the Secretary-General to close out the peacekeeping operation ... And with no irony intended, the resolution also underscored the contribution of the UN to the past four years of peace. But can a four year lull in the fighting be considered an accomplishment when both sides simply use it to re-arm?

Further, strategies tended to reiterate Western conceptions of progress and development – trading on the universality of liberalism and internationally driven market relations – and to conceptualize pre-existing social, political, and economic forms as problematic, or even nonexistent. To this extent, the UN tended to ignore informal political and economic systems to the point where one could get the impression that they simply did not exist at all. This mode of thinking lent credibility to UN programmes designed to extend liberal structures of governance, property title, and citizenship, but was implicitly reliant upon the notion that communities had no political will or decision-making mechanisms and, in effect, village people lived in "a state of nature". In Uige this assumption was proven quite obviously false.

Similarly, the UN mission engaged primarily with the "legitimate" government, and therefore, within UN narrativized spaces, the conflict was depicted overwhelmingly as a top-down struggle to suppress "illegitimate" rebel and warlord forces with diminishing, if any, domestic support (again I speak systemically and not about the views of individual staff members in Angola). However, while I was confined to MPLA-held areas – and within this space Angola's people were officially represented as largely MPLA supporters held hostage by the fierce, brutal, and belligerent UNITA terrorism – casual conversations with local staff revealed that all was not as it seemed. Many felt that support for UNITA was still strong. That said, no one professed to be a UNITA supporter themselves. Nevertheless, continuing UNITA support would indicate a domestic depth to the struggle that has tended to be marginalized in many contemporary accounts.

Ultimately, however, there are undoubtedly narratives which I did not perceive, but, rather, took as objective. Unfortunately during this field research, I did not spend enough time outside UN narrativized spaces to get a firm grasp on what those might be. I am currently working on implementing a second phase in which I would work with an NGO over a longer period of time in order to overcome some of the constraints mentioned above.

Interview ethics and strategies

As noted, the research window was time-bound, and consisted of only one month in Angola, split between the northern province of Uige and Luanda. This meant, however, that I had limited time and opportunity to build trust and inter-subjective understandings with local people. Therefore, I confined the substantive interview process to UN and government officials. This made sense within the context of my research project, but there were also a number of other reasons for this.

The first, and I believe most important, was the fact that my research offered local people very limited to non-existent rewards. By talking to me, life would not necessarily be better. They would not necessarily understand themselves, the war, or the UN engagement better. They would not increase their earning power, self-esteem, or access to limited resources. The benefits would not be concrete or tangible. Further, members of the international community were seen, at least in Uige, to have enormous power: they could, potentially, result in a person getting on the WFP distribution list; they could undertake to provide immediate medical care; and they could organize medical, building, or food supplies from abroad. They could see that streams were rehabilitated, children were schooled, and "internally displaced persons" (IDPs) were sheltered. None of these desperately needed goods and services was likely to be even the most indirect result of my research. Raising the spectre of such hopes seemed to be quite unethical.

I did, however, conduct interviews with the UNHCR IDP camp residents as part of a report I was preparing for Luanda. At this time, I recorded a tragic story of a village that had been attacked, allegedly by the FAA (government troops); the leader and elders were shot, and the rest of the village was forcibly displaced to Uige. Interviews with the military commander confirmed the general thrust of events, but claimed that elders were shot in crossfire between UNITA troops, and that villagers had been evacuated for their own safety. The villagers rejected the claim of UNITA presence and insisted they be allowed to return to their tribal lands and subsistence crops. It was clear that they desperately wanted to return, and they were imploring me to speak on their behalf. Their conception of the power I wielded was profoundly exaggerated, I believe, and while I did enter their plight into the report, having no time or capacity to follow up with the progress of their case made this interview a deeply ethically problematic event, especially given the profundity of their loss and the life-long implications entailed by being denied return to their lands.

Another problem with relying only on superficially contextualized interviews with war-affected populations is that the researcher may not have enough time to gauge the political climate and the ramifications of the information they document. Vivid descriptions of illegal or informal survival strategies, or controversial views of the conflict, or even subversive activities, may provide clues on how to promote or suppress these activities, thereby further endangering the marginalized and peripheralized people (Chingono, unpublished).

Finally, war-affected populations may have only a fragmented sense of the conflict, and rely on highly mythologized cultural symbols to explain the dominance of fear and uncertainty. In Uige, this appeared to manifest as a pervasive sense of otherworldly evil in their midst – often resulting in violent interpersonal confrontation. However, without an in-depth study of its function, the complexity, nuance, and rationality of witchcraft as a hedge against uncertainty can easily be lost in the ethnocentric rush to dismiss the African cultures as savage and irrational *others* (Chabal, 1997).

Thus, I chose to concentrate on interviews with the international community and MPLA government officials. The first problem with this was the inability to access UNITA officials. This was partially corrected by interviews with MPLA officials who were former UNITA members, and sympathetic to UNITA's ideals and the official UNITA website. It did mean, however, that all spaces I visited in Angola were MPLA/UN sites with their multi-layered narrative spaces.

There were a number of ethical advantages to this approach. UN and government officials are savvy and understand, by and large, research processes, the structures of incentive and reward that researchers face and the intangibility of research contributions. Further, the power relationship between officials and me was relatively equal or skewed in their favour. Finally, I do not speak Portuguese, but English and French, as commensurate with ten years French immersion. Generally, then, while I did rely on a translator on several occasions, in Luanda I could often interview in English, and in Uige, given the historical relationship between northern Angola and south-western Democratic Republic of Congo, I was able to conduct a number of interviews in French.

Conclusion

Sustaining domination-based power relations generally involves the maintenance of existing social structures and the institutions that support them. Conversely, challenges from below can be expressed by creating new structures and patterns of interaction that make the supposedly powerless less dependent upon the requirements and rules of those trying to dominate them (Bell, 1999: 104).

This chapter has highlighted a number of themes and conclusions that emerged out of – while also informing – my approach to the literature review and the field research. Most important are the issues of subjectivity and the politics of truth, and how these impart a *flavour* to power, that may in fact, cause policies and strategies designed in the first instance to contain or resolve conflict, to create or exacerbate it.

Informed by these perspectives, research – including field research – branched off from any pretensions to re-evaluate the truth claims embedded in competing analyses of the Angolan conflict, or to spokespersons on behalf of Angolans. Rather, it takes as its cue the marked exclusion of Angolans from all the important decisions about the trajectories of their lives, their communities, and their networked spaces, and seeks to illuminate the pregnant conflict in exclusion, the interests served by exclusion, and how that nexus of power reproduces itself.

Note

1. Foucault makes access to the production of truth an important feature of emancipatory politics. It may also be an important feature of conflict. When access is quite limited, truth is reproduced in the context of "deep conflict". That is, "a deep conflict is a conflict where there are no procedures or structures to which parties involved in a conflict can appeal" (Haugaard, 1999: 119). In a situation of deep conflict, levels of coercion will tend to be high, and the risk of unstructured or violent conflict is high. This is, I believe, a good explanation of why desperate and disparate Angolans took up arms against the Portuguese in the revolts beginning in 1961. A more "superficial conflict" is one where shared structures of conflict resolution exist. Trading on the reflexivity of knowledge, then, I take the theoretical hypothesis that institutions can be reordered, and unstructured conflict can be transformed into structured conflict where sufficiently open and flexible institutions for structural consensus building and rebuilding can be effected. "Once this has been done, compromise between conflicting groups is, at least potentially, possible because structural consensus can be used to convert violence into structurally-based exercises of power" (Haugaard, 1999: 119). Notably, "power" here stands for empowerment, and not power over.

REFERENCES

Abrahamsen, Rita (2000) *Disciplining Democracy*, London and New York: Zed Books.

Adibe, Clement (1998) "Accepting external authority in peace-maintenance", *Global Governance* 4(1): 107–122.

Bell, Nancy (1999) "Power, Alternative Theories of", *Encyclopedia of Violence, Peace and Conflict*, San Diego, London, Boston, New York, Sydney, Tokyo, Toronto: Academic Press, pp. 99–105.

Bodely, John, (1994) *Cultural Anthropology: Tribes, States, and the Global System*, London, Toronto, California: Mayfield Publishing.

Brown, Chris (1999) "Universal human rights: a critique", in Tim Dunne and Nicholas Wheeler, eds., *Human Rights in Global Politics*, Cambridge: Cambridge University Press, pp. 103–127.

Chabal, Patrick (1997) *Apocalypse Now? A Postcolonial Journey into Africa*, www.kcl.ac.uk/depsta/humanities/pobrst/pcpapers.htm.

Chopra, Jaret, ed. (1998) *The Politics of Peace Maintenance*, Boulder, Colo.: Lynne Rienner.

Charlesworth, Hillary (1993) "Alienating Oscar? Feminist analysis of international law", in Henry Steiner and Philip Alston, eds., *International Human Rights in Context: Law, Politics, Morality*, Oxford/New York: Oxford University Press.

Chingono, Mark, "Reflections on Wartime Social Research: Lessons from the Mozambican Civil War", unpublished.

Clapham, Christopher (1998) "Being peacekept", in Oliver Furley and Roy May, eds., *Peacekeeping in Africa*, Aldershot: Ashgate.

Clausewitz, Carl von (1976) *On War*, trans. Michael Howard and Peter Paret, Princeton: Princeton University Press.

Cox, Robert (1981) "Social forces, states, and world orders: beyond international relations theory", *Millennium: Journal of International Studies* 10(2): 126–155.

Davidson, Basil (1975) *In the Eye of the Storm: Angola's People*, Harmondsworth: Penguin Books.

Delanty, Gerald (1997) *Social Science: Beyond Constructivism and Realism*, Minneapolis: University of Minnesota Press.

Duffield, Mark (2001) *Global Governance and the New Wars*, London/New York: Zed Books.

Foucault, Michel (1997) *Ethics, Subjectivity and Truth*, ed., Paul Rabinow, New York: New Press.

Grovogui, Siba N'Zatioula (1996) *Sovereigns, Quasi Sovereigns, and Africans*, Minneapolis, London: University of Minnesota Press.

Harding, Jeremy (1993) *Small Wars, Small Mercies*, London: Viking.

Haugaard, Mark (1999) "Power, social and political theories of", in *Encyclopedia of Peace and Conflict*, Burlington, MA: Academic Press.

Heywood, Linda (2000) *Contested Power in Angola, 1840s to the Present*, Rochester: University of Rochester Press.

Hodges, Tony (2001) *Angola from Afro-Stalinism to Petro-Diamond Capitalism*, Bloomington IN: Indiana University Press.

Jett, Dennis (1999) *Why Peacekeeping Fails*, London: Palgrave.

Malaquias, Assis (2000) "Ethnicity and conflict in Angola: prospects for reconciliation", in Jakkie Cilliers and Christian Dietrich, eds., *Angola's War Economy*, South Africa: Institute for Security Studies.

Marks, Susan (2000) *The Riddle of all Constitutions*, New York: Oxford University Press.

Minter, William (1994) *Apartheid's Contrast*, Johannesburg: Witwatersrand University Press and London/New York: Zed Books.

Pratchett, Terry (2001) *The Truth*, London: Corgi Adult Books.

Reno, William (1998) *Warlord Politics and African State*, Boulder, Colo./London: Lynne Rienner.

Ruggie, Gerald (1998) "What makes the world hang together? Neo-utilitarianism and the social constructivist challenge", *International Organisation* 52(4): 855–885.

Sogge, David (2000) "Angola: the client who came in from the cold", *Southern Africa Report* 15(4): 4–6.

Thakur, Ramesh (1999) "United Nations and human security", *Canadian Foreign Policy* 7(1): 51–59.

United Nations (2000) Report of the Panel on United Nations Peace Operations, A/55/305 S/2000/809.

9

Gender research in violently divided societies: Methods and ethics of "international" researchers in Rwanda

Erin K. Baines

In September 2000 I was requested to join a team of researchers to conduct a programme review of the UN Rwandan Women's Initiative (RWI) by the Women's Commission for Refugee Women and Children (WCRWC) and the co-ordinating body of the RWI, the UN High Commissioner for Refugees (UNHCR). Initiated in 1997, the RWI was one of three women's initiatives in Rwanda[1] designed to "empower" women in post-genocide Rwanda. Projects spanned from macro-level legal and policy changes to micro-level income generation, housing, and psycho-social care. The results of my findings were to provide feedback into UNHCR's overall strategy to empower refugee women in post-conflict settings. To achieve this, a workshop was held with all stake-holders (the UN, the Government of National Unity (GNU), and members of the women's umbrella group *Profemme*), at the end of the six-week review. The review included archival searches of background and concept papers, email exchanges and status reports, as well as inter-views with past and present UNHCR staff involved in the initiative, national and local government officials, representatives of women's organizations and associations, and finally, beneficiaries themselves. Data interpretation involved a consultative approach with women's organizations, the GNU and UNHCR officials in Kigali, Geneva, and Washington DC.

The RWI review was one of hundreds of reviews and evaluations con-ducted on the subject of women and violently divided societies in the past ten years. "Gender audits" and gender-sensitive programme reviews are a response to the perceived need to design humanitarian policies and

140

programmes that address gender-related experiences of women as well as men. However, I am concerned that little emphasis has been given to methods and ethics in such reviews. In addition, the drive to highlight women and apply gender analysis in relation to such programmes sometimes obscures complex dynamics within the violently divided societies, such as wider political and economic contexts, but also the intersections of ethnicity, age, or class with gender.

In this chapter, I reflect upon dual roles I have assumed as an academic and programme reviewer of women's projects. In each role, I have been exposed to different bodies of literature dealing with methods and ethics (gender analyses of humanitarian operations and feminist methods). These two bodies of literature are largely discrete, but, nonetheless, they could and should inform each other. To this end, I employ these two bodies of literature to conduct a "lessons learned" approach of the RWI programme review.

Background on gender research

With the onset of crises in the Balkans, Rwanda, and Somalia, as well as more protracted conflicts in Afghanistan, Angola, and Sudan, international spending on relief increased rapidly during the 1990s. During the same period, domestic concerns regarding inflated deficits and high taxation ushered in the government practice of "results-based management", characterized by a preoccupation with efficiency and desire for greater transparency and accountability in government spending. International spending has come under particularly close scrutiny, and the burden has fallen upon multilateral and bilateral donor agencies to illustrate results (Crisp, 2000: 4–7). Today, evaluations are considered a central aspect of promoting accountability to people caught within conflict situations, and the desire of the international community to move towards a culture of learning to improve current operations. Methods and ethics have become fashionable where major bilateral and multilateral humanitarian and development agencies have produced comprehensive sets of guidelines on conducting needs assessment and evaluations of their programmes.[2] Generally, these guides reflect Western donor preoccupations with results-based management, and detail an array of helpful ways of differentiating objectives, activities, outputs, outcomes, and impacts. To promote learning, emphasis is placed on generating the interests of stakeholders in the evaluation process, as well as on the importance of consulting with stakeholders on evaluation results and methods for dispersing results. Ethically, guidelines tend to focus on the need for balanced research teams (most often by sex or geography, noting most evaluators tend to be Western and male), and accountability to the persons researched through participatory methods (recognizing that research tends to take a high-level, objective approach excluding people involved).

Gender analysis and feminist methods have received scant attention in these guidelines.[3] Thus, whilst useful information on how to conduct evaluations now is readily available, gender differentials within programmes are not taken into consideration. Moreover, gender analysis generally was not considered as relevant within "standard" evaluations of programmes.

In the 1990s, there was a surge in gender analyses on the subject of women in armed conflict/post-conflict settings. Anticipating and responding to the call for more "woman-relevant" research in violently divided societies in Critical Area E of the Beijing Platform for Action (1995) and the Security Council Resolution 1325 on Women, Peace and Security (2000), a wide spectrum of studies have begun to document the gendered impact of armed conflict on women, gender-related protection needs, the challenges of exile and refuge for refugee and internally displaced women, the challenges of reconstruction, and the particular plight of girls during armed conflict (see, for example, Amnesty International, 1995; Copelon, 1995; Forbes Martin, 1992; Human Rights Watch, 1997; Turshen and Twagiramariya, 1998; also the report sections on the UNIFEM and WCRWC websites). Fewer reports have extended this focus to include the specific gender-related needs of men and boys in armed conflict, where men and boys are targeted because of their gender, or where programmes might overlook their particular needs based on an assumed gender norm (for example, programmes to assist victims of sexual violence often fail to engage men either as perpetrators or victims themselves) (Turner, 1999).

To ensure UN and bilateral responsibility to men and women equally, women's rights organizations and activists have accumulated a good deal of research on how specific programmes exclude women based on assumptions of neutrality. For instance, the WCRWC, an international NGO, has conducted programme reviews and evaluations of UNHCR since the release of its Policy on Refugee Women, to ensure the policy and guidelines are adhered to in field operations of the organization. In 2001, the agency undertook an extensive comparative analysis of policy implementation in five UNHCR field offices. More strategically, gender analyses also seek to underscore the agency of women, to highlight their contributions and relative importance to realizing aid effectiveness. For example, a number of important reports now exist on the topic of "women's roles" in peace-building and highlight areas for programme intervention to support women's efforts (see, for example, Corrin, 2001; Porter, 2003; UNESCO, 1998; UNIFEM, 2001; UNHCR et al., 1998).

These gender works are important in bringing "women" into view, but troublingly, few gender analyses outline methods and ethics of conducting research on the topic. So, while standard evaluations tend to marginalize gender analysis, gender analyses of women in conflict and humanitarian responses tend to marginalize the relevance of reflecting upon methods. To consider how humanitarian evaluations and reviews might become more inclusive of gender and women, I briefly examine feminist academic and cross-disciplinary methodologies, and then quickly move onto more recent arguments regarding the need to move beyond gender and incorporate a diversity lens when researching "women" in violently divided societies.

First, while diverse[4] feminist methodologists tend to deliberately focus on gender, and emphasize emancipatory goals: "feminist research must be part of a process by which women's oppression is not only described but challenged" (Kirsh, 1999: 3), feminist methods tend to be qualitative, rejecting positivist assumptions about "neutral" or "objective" knowledge. As such, they are often charged with subjectivity and flawed, but contend that as the world is socially constructed anyway, there is no such thing as a neutral researcher.[5] If it is socially constructed, then careful research can point to ways it can be reconstructed.

Collaboration with participants in research generally is considered both ethical and necessary methodologically, so that learning can be mutually beneficial, interactive and cooperative. In her participant-observation study of mixed ethnic women's groups working for peace in Northern Ireland, Bosnia-Herzegovina, and Israel and Palestine, Cynthia Cockburn (1999) employed a method of collaboration throughout all stages of her research project: she consulted groups on the research design, findings, and in the write-up of results. As a result, Cockburn was able to gain the trust of women working within these groups, to try to grasp how they worked together in and across differences, despite enormous pressures and constraints working against them. She was able to draw a number of conclusions that potentially serve as a *Good Practice* criteria, and measurement for gender analysts.

Nevertheless, a great deal of Western feminist research on "Third World women" problematically has lumped together a widely differentiated group, and characterized it as downtrodden and disadvantaged next to the presumably liberated Western woman. Moreover, Western feminist methods for gathering information on Third World women reproduce the positivist tendency to objectify and colonize, where women caught in conflict come under the gaze of Western researchers and are represented perniciously as the overly oppressed "other" in need of rescue by Western women and men.[6] Charges that such representations lead to programmes and policies that are more about "Western" women, than

"Third World" women, have been levied, exposing neocolonialist tendencies when gender "experts" have made their careers off their "Third World" sisters' backs (see Marchand and Parpart, 1995). Nevertheless, gender analysis remains an important avenue of investigation, albeit researchers are reminded that they should not privilege gender. It is to the methods and episteme that one might find ways of overcoming neocolonial tendencies, and open up the discussion to look at and yet go beyond gender considerations.

Post-colonial feminist methods challenge the power-riddled relationship between researchers and the researched, calling upon researchers to reflect upon their own subject positions, and how these shape the research process and agenda. As England (1994) suggests, reflexivity is fundamental to fieldwork, as it involves self-critical scrutiny of the self as researcher, which in turn, can prompt unexpected insights and new ideas about research questions.

Research reflexivity promotes a more flexible approach to the research agenda, incorporating perhaps unanticipated findings, difficulties in the research process, and "silences" that might otherwise be dismissed in positivist approaches. Such an approach requires me, as a Western researcher, to reflect upon my own assumptions during a programme review such as the one I did in Rwanda, where I evaluated projects on the basis of my own definitions, with little consultation with Rwandan women's organizations beforehand. At one point, the regional adviser for gender suggested that my concept of basic human needs, democracy, and rights were Western-centric and needed to be placed in an "African" context. I might also look at some of the silences generated during my research and what those silences meant. For instance, it was not infrequent that rural women fell silent when I asked them about the projects they were involved with. Informal discussions with representatives from women's organizations revealed that these silences were due largely to the fact the projects had failed, or in fact did not materialize at all, and the women were reluctant to say so in front of the RWI focal point that accompanied me. I might also interpret this silence as a form of fear, where any criticism of the government-run programme might have resulted in harm. Here, too, I was reminded that gender, ethnicity, and class were variables that shaped the limits of possibility and opportunity for Rwandan women, where recipient and aid providers, urban and rural women, Hutu and Tutsi women exist in power relations with one another.

The post-colonial critique raises difficult ethical dilemmas for gender researchers and on the question of representation:

The politics of interpretation and representation are particularly vexing for feminist researchers because they so often hope to empower the people they study and to improve the conditions of their lives. Yet, inevitably, researchers are implicated in the process of speaking for others, potentially silencing them. And in this silence, representation can become misrepresentation, the reinforcement of unjust power structures and institutional hierarchies. But the effort to make feminist research emancipatory, non-hierarchical, mutually beneficial, and collaborative raises some critical questions. How can we ever know (and predict) whether the results of a research study will benefit women – that is, whether it is truly for women? Who chooses emancipatory goals and why? Whose desire is it to empower? What does the desire to empower others say about researchers? Unless we learn to ask these questions and become reflective and self-critical, we are in danger of imposing our desires, our goals, and our worldview upon others, despite our best intentions (Kirsh, 1999: 47).

A common method to avoid the potential paralysis of representation is to open a process of dialogue between the researcher and the researched (see Alcoff, 1998; Parpart, 1995; Uvin, 2001). This is as basic as consulting with "people" and not just policy-makers and government representatives. It also means adopting methods for opening up communication where the process of dialogue is not in itself a neutral process. I was involved in the Global Dialogue with Refugee Women, where 50 refugee and internally displaced women met and conversed with senior managers in Geneva, Switzerland. This was the first time refugees had had the opportunity to dialogue directly with high-level officials, and it was fascinating to see how the methods for promoting dialogue shaped that process. For example, the workshop method was left open deliberately so that refugee women could identify and discuss what was important to them.

Post-colonial feminists, in order to displace the authority of the researcher and affirm the integrity of the researched in the written text, have explored alternative means of presenting research findings. For example, some analyses have used "multivocal" text, including more than one author's interpretation of the data. Another method is to present lengthy quotations from interviews with the researched within texts to promote the "voices of the marginalized" or to simply record oral histories, with as little interference and interpretation by the researcher. The latter is, in fact, a favoured strategy of advocates for women in conflict and post-conflict zones, where a number of texts and reports centre on the voices of women, their experiences of war told by their voices. In this move, women are not objects of study, but subjects, authorities of knowledge. It has been interesting to see how those in high-level policy positions receive this type of text. In my experience, they either charge the author(s) with illegitimacy because the report is too subjective, too emotive, or, when "women's voices" are not captured adequately in text, I have heard officials argue that reports are too unrepresentative of "real people" and therefore not authentic.

Ethically, feminist methods are appealing in terms of collaborative research, being reflective of the impact of their work, and seeking ways to disrupt power relations that are oppressive to research subjects. Methodologically, the distinction between ethical and epistemological becomes more blurred; such methods potentially provide more context-rich analysis by situating research subjects in their everyday lives and collecting data that specifically seeks to reflect the participants' perspectives. Collaboration on setting the research agenda and interpreting data is more likely to focus on knowledge relevant to participants (than to researchers). In addition, collaboration promotes a degree of credibility among participants, thereby opening up new sources of information within the community. This brief review of gender analyses in violently divided societies and academic musings on methods and ethics sets the stage for reflecting on lessons learned in my own participation in the review of the RWI.

Lessons learned: methods and ethics of conducting programme reviews of women's projects in post-conflict settings

As the following lessons learned will illustrate, much of my research work in Rwanda was a "learn by doing" experience. In the following, I reflect candidly about this experience and incorporate aspects of the methods outlined in the previous sections to suggest ways of improving current methods of researching women and using gender analysis in violently divided societies. Such lessons generally fall into one of three interrelated dimensions, all infused with power, as identified by Diane Wolf (1996: 2):

First, power differences stemming from different positionalities of the researcher and researched ...; second, power exerted during the research process, such as defining the research relationship, unequal exchange, and exploitation; and third, power exerted during the post-fieldwork period – writing and representation.

The research team

The research team should be a coordinated and non-hierarchical balance of "insiders" and "outsiders", recognizing that differences infused with power exist between both "insiders" and "outsiders", as well as between "outsiders/insiders". In the RWI review, I was one of two external researchers that worked in collaboration with UNHCR staff, the Government of National Unity, and representatives of women's organizations.

However, the research team broke down considerably over the course of planning, where communication and coordination between researchers located in Ottawa, New York, Geneva, Kigali, and Kenya proved difficult. As a result of miscommunication, members of the team arrived and departed at different times during the intended three-and-a-half-week review in Rwanda. This resulted in differing perspectives and interpretations of the review's objectives, expectations of what could be done, and interpretation of data, and it aggravated levels of authority between insiders and outsiders on the team.

Identity is an extremely sensitive issue in all violently divided societies, and Rwanda is no exception. The team was composed mainly of an external researcher (myself), a "new caseload returnee" (the translator) and "old caseload returnees" (the RWI focal point and a representative of the Ministry for Women and Gender Equality). At varying times, members of *Profemme* joined the team, as did a Spanish programme officer from Headquarters in Geneva, and the regional gender adviser from Kenya. Not much thought was given originally to the composition of this team in terms of sex, geography, or ethnicity. It became obvious over time that the RWI focal point had an affiliation with the GNU, and that her presence in many of the interviews with women's organizations and associations was a reminder to interviewees of the GNU position, and I believe this made women uncomfortable. Moreover, as we depended on the RWI focal point and old caseload returnees from *Profemme* and the Ministry for Women and Gender to help organize the review, we were directed therefore towards beneficiaries who had had a positive experience, and most of these women were survivors (Tutsi women). This did not permit the team to examine failed projects, or women generally excluded from such projects, such as new caseload returnees (Hutu women).

Other chapters in this collection discuss the relative merits of "outsiders" and "insiders" in conducting research in violently divided societies, and so I will limit my comments to the following advantages and disadvantages that I perceived in the Rwandan case. First, as an "outsider" I had a limited understanding of the socio-historical and political context of Rwandans, and could not pick up on the cultural cues and exchanges in the Kinyarwandan language and tradition. This led to a great deal of frustration on my own behalf and that of the other team members, as I was always trying to "catch-up" on events and dialogue. On the other hand, I was perhaps granted the "space" required to ask difficult or sensitive questions to local authorities that "insiders" could not. I felt in the final workshop that this trade-off was revealed transparently when women's groups urged me to speak critically of the GNU and RWI, a practice they felt unable to do themselves.

The research agenda and collecting information

A shared understanding of the objectives of the review or evaluation must be negotiated and agreed upon by different stakeholders involved. A consultative approach to developing research questions and methods should be taken, with sensitivity to local contexts and gender relations. During the planning of my research trip, different members of the team used the term "review" or "evaluation", attaching a different set of expectations to each. Review implied a historical description of activities, procedures, and achievements to date, whereas evaluation referred to a more in-depth, impact assessment of projects. The difference in emphasis raised different expectations in UNHCR and *Profemme*, where actors were disappointed about how much the research team could achieve in the given time-frame and at times this disappointment translated into decreased respect and legitimacy for the team. Beneficiaries of projects were not well prepared on the reasons for our visit. Grassroots women viewed my presence as a funding opportunity, and I was often presented with a "wish list". It took considerable time to explain I was conducting a review for an international advocacy organization, which could only act to lobby donors. All of this later raised the question about what the research agenda should look like, what information should be gathered and how it should be written up.

The review employed a range of different questionnaires, but met with the challenge of interviewing a diversity of actors, all with differing subject positions and relations to the RWI. These questions were based largely on UNHCR programme reports and they largely addressed the matters relating to process. Yet the questions did not always make sense in the context of the interviewed that had varying knowledge about the RWI process. I often found it advantageous to abandon the survey and ask questions based on "gut instincts". My field notes thus consisted of pages of notes to be organized and reviewed later, trying to make sense of what was communicated to me by the translator. Given limited time constraints, I did not attempt to collect quantitative data, although it is interesting to note that readers of the report requested statistics, arguing that such data would help legitimize the findings of the study.

I will also emphasize the importance of interviewing women separately from men. When I attempted to interview men and women in mixed groups regarding the impact of RWI, men dominated conversations, and women were reluctant to speak in the presence of men. I also recall an instance in Mostar, Bosnia-Herzegovina (BiH) when I visited a rural community and was seated at a table with men while women busily prepared coffee for us. I had to get up and work with the women to ask them questions about the project designed to assist them in their day-to-day chores. Sometimes, it is the case that women are not used to public speaking, and are shy to play this role. I also recall an evaluation with returnee Guatemalan women where men insisted on answering question-naires, believing that their wives were totally unable to do so. Having said this, many external analyses of women's projects focus their inter-views exclusively with women, and fail to interview men at all. This is problematic also, given that very often the successes of "women's empowerment projects" are conditioned by the attitudes of men in the home and community. For example, in Tuzla, BiH, I interviewed men and women separately about a cow distribution project intended to improve women's income and choices. Men proclaimed how great the project was, while women pointed out that it had only increased their workload, as they had to hand the money generated over to their husbands.

Analysing data

To analyse data, a participatory approach that consults research subjects should be sought. Authors should reflect upon their own roles in shaping the research agenda. Workshops that involve the researched in the interpretation of data are helpful. The final workshop with the GNU, women's organizations, and UNHCR was invaluable in terms of affirming my observations and adding new perspectives. Engaging all three actors was productive insofar as it was important to promote communication between them; however, in future I would hold three separate workshops with each set of actors before bringing them together. The three had very different interests in the findings of the review, and the different power relations among them possibly silenced some actors. With the assistance of the WCRWC, I also engaged UNHCR (mostly senior-level) officials in Kigali, or who had been in Kigali previously, in a discussion of my find-ings, often following up personally on their recommendations. I believe this strategy helped promote ownership and legitimacy within UNHCR, where ultimately policy decisions are taken.

Gender analysis in context

Gender relations and roles should be situated within political and eco-nomic contexts of the region, country or community, and understood to exist in relation to (and constituted by) race, ethnicity, class, ability or sex-ual orientation. The terms of reference for the review of the RWI speci-fied that I should identify and document good practices, and illustrate how international organizations, through specific initiatives, could contri-bute to women's empowerment and peace-building. However, women's projects tend to be marginalized within overall humanitarian pro-grammes. Likewise, evaluations tend to focus on the impact of specific projects outside the wider programme efforts. For example, while in Geneva I met a key UNHCR official responsible for the Great Lakes region. While this person could provide me with substantive information on UN programmes in Rwanda, the representative admitted outright to knowing little about the RWI.

Conversely, existing RWI reports focused on the specificities of projects, without relating them to the wider political-economic context within which they operated. So, while I had a good picture of the impact of housing projects for women, I was provided with little information on general housing projects for the public, and whether or not the women's project made a difference to standard practices. In another example, I was assured that RWI supported the efforts of women to engage in political life and the economy, and to secure their rights in post-genocide Rwanda. RWI sponsored the creation of women's committees in each commune and prefecture, a supposed means of inserting women's voices into male-dominated local and national authorities. Yet regrettably, I was afforded little opportunity to investigate the impact of women's committees on decision-making in such structures. Let me make my point in another example: I have read at least four separate international reports on successful interventions to promote Burundian women's voices in the Arusha peace process. Little analysis has been done to ask what impact this actually has had on the process of peace, or for the women involved. Likewise, while there have been a good number of internationally sponsored women's and peace initiatives in Rwanda, gender analyses of these efforts generally fail to situate women's efforts to promote peace in the larger security concerns that characterize the region. Finally, attribution between international interventions and impacts on Burundian women's lives is not clear in these reports.

More troubling was the fact that my pre-occupation with gender displaced a focus on differences and power relations among women. It has been noted by Diane Wolf (1996) that gender advocates often essentialize women in a strategic manner, in order to promote women's empowerment. For instance, women often are characterized as apolitical and "more peaceful" than men, and often this justifies international support to them in post-conflict settings. It is also a strategic move, where work with women becomes possible in a divided society based on the stereotype that they are not actors with vested interests. Yet:

In Rwandan politics today it matters what a person's (presumed) ethnic background is, where that person lived in Rwanda, and where that person came from if he or she is an exile who came home after the genocide. Understanding these distinctions can be critical to understanding the dynamics within and among women's organizations. Although Rwandan women have displayed a remarkable capacity to transcend differences and work together, distinctions based on ethnicity, class, region, place of origin, and life experiences remain salient (Newbury and Baldwin, 2000: 10).

At the end of my research trip, I had only just begun to understand the dynamics at play: as I have already pointed out, RWI projects tended to target survivors of the genocide and old caseload returnees tended to manage these projects. New caseload returnees usually were excluded altogether, or at the very least were involved on the terms of the government and forced to assume the discourse of the new Rwandan national unity. Urban-educated women also tended to benefit disproportionately to uneducated rural women, where resources were concentrated in Kigali. Tensions among women based on perceived ethnic and class differences were exacerbated potentially by the RWI, yet the entire initiative soundly denied the existence of differences, reflecting the GNU position that "all Rwandans were equal". Yet they are, in fact, not all equal. In this sense, internationals and national elites had an interest in highlighting the relevance of gender, to the detriment of exploring other sources of discrimination Rwandan women might face. Again this is not to say gender is unimportant, but rather to emphasize that gender discrimination is shaped by ethnic, class, and other forms of social differences and discrimination.

Accountability

It is essential to provide those "being researched" with the final "product" of the research. This is sometimes challenging given poor communication or postal services, and if face-to-face follow-ups through workshops are not possible. I encountered a number of persons reluctant to speak with me as they argued that Western researchers tended to take up their time and then simply disappear with the information. As Peter Uvin (2001) has argued, "international" researchers with the privilege and ability to move in and out of violently divided societies must be accountable to persons from whom they gather information, and on the basis of which life and death decisions will be made. A number of participants in RWI research urged me to lobby the WCRWC and UN to translate the report into French or Kinyarwandan to promote greater accessibility to the report.

Ethics

People who are researched should be treated like people and not as mere mines of information to be exploited. Collaboration between researcher and researched is potentially one means of avoiding exploitative relationships, particularly where "the researched" are saturated by well-meaning researchers. I think many graduate students have enthusiastically started their research, only to be met with extreme scepticism by organizations or groups whom they seek to "study", learning quickly that they are not the first to pursue the subject. I am reminded here of my own doctoral research in Guatemala, where on some days I bumped into more graduate students than I did Guatemalans.

I have also seen this phenomenon in the humanitarian assistance world, where popular issues such as war-affected children have been "over-studied" in some countries, and where objects of study are indeed exploited – programmers leave perhaps with a good note for the file or funding proposal, graduate students return to earn their doctorate, and the researched are often left with nothing. As discussed in the previous sections, there are ways to avoid this, such as collaborative research, where an exchange is established at the outset: for example, my work with Guatemalan women's organizations in Canada involved participant observation, where I not only learned valuable information, but also contributed to proposal writing, awareness-raising campaigns, and fundraising. In Rwanda, I relied on the women's network *Profemme* to carry out most of my work with women's associations. They requested I work with them on their project indicators and in retrospect, this could have been an initiative built into the programme review.

On constraints

All research in violently divided societies or elsewhere should recognize the limits of the possible, and seek to move beyond them. There are a number of constraints shaping the research methods of international humanitarian and development organizations or advocacy groups. First, the "tyranny of emergency" generally is cited as one of the main reasons that humanitarian workers[1] fail to conduct any analysis, much less gender analysis. Complex emergencies, and in the case of Rwanda this state lasted up to three years, mean conditions are always changing and that humanitarian actors perceive the need to act quickly to save lives. Yet many studies have argued that this is precisely the time to conduct gender-sensitive assessments, where thinking about gender from the start helps to correct many of the negative impacts women encounter later on (such as setting up camps, food programmes, and so on). I think we need to work more carefully through the issue of time in conducting research, where long-term ethnographic research often is not possible, or where the amount of time the "international" researcher spends in the field drains resources from civil society and humanitarian workers.

Second, it is important to consider that institutional cultures value some types of knowledge over others. It is perhaps not so much the need for more knowledge, but to question whose knowledge is valued. Thus gender advocates insist on the value of "listening" to the women caught in conflict and not solely to the male leadership. However, beyond this, decision-makers and policy-makers within the higher echelons of the UN or bilateral donors tend to value their own knowledge over that of persons within conflict, despite the fact that they are removed from that area. New methods might unearth indigenous knowledge (such as participant observation or collaborative methods), but mechanisms for bringing this knowledge "up" to decision-makers, or decision-making "down" to persons in conflict zones/post-conflict settings are required.

Conclusions: What is at stake?

There is always a potential to "do more harm" (Anderson 1999) than good when researching violently divided societies, and in the production of research results. As such, methods and ethics of conducting research should figure prominently on any research agenda in this context, and therefore it is alarming that relatively little attention is paid to this topic in gender analyses of conflict/post-conflict settings. I recently attended a high-level (government and UN) meeting on integrating a conflict-prevention strategy into development approaches, where knowledge production and sharing emerged as an unofficial theme. I left this meeting with the distinct impression that we can expect more research, not less, to take place in violently divided societies. I believe that gender analysis can help to reveal how men and women experience violence and respond to the challenges it poses differently, but that these experiences must not be examined as if they take place in a vacuum, as presented frequently in gender analyses and texts. Post-colonial critiques reveal some of the inherent ethical and methodological dilemmas in conducting research, as well as alternatives to break down hierarchies of knowledge or the privileging of some knowledge over others. To this end, researchers should consider "unveiling" themselves in the process of performing research, to ask "who are we for them?" and "who are they for us" (Bell, Caplan and Karim, 1993: 34). Doing so begins to chip away at previously held assumptions about the potential of research, and reveal new ways of thinking and doing research on more ethical and reciprocal bases.

Notes

1. Two other initiatives were USAID's Women in Transition Initiative and UNDP's Trust Fund for Women.
2. See, for example, evaluation websites at: United Nations Children's Fund (UNICEF), Research and Evaluation, http://www.unicef.org/reseval/; United Nations High Commission for Refugees; UNHCR, Evaluation and Planning, http://www.unhcr.ch/evaluate/links.htm; United Nations Educational, Scientific and Cultural Organization, (UNESCO); Bureaux for Strategic Planning, http://www.unesco.org/bpe/bpe_en/index.htm; The World Bank, Evaluation Monitoring and Quality Enhancement, http://www.worldbank.org/html/oed/evaluation/; Canadian International Development Association (CIDA), Evaluation Unit, http://www.acdi-cida.gc.ca/perfor-e.htm; International Research and Development Centre (IDRC); Evaluation Unit, http://www.idrc.ca/evaluation/index_e.html.
3. In the winter of 2000 I was commissioned by the Status of Women Canada to review current evaluation methods from a gender perspective, and so make this observation based on this work.
4. Feminist empiricist, stand-point, and postmodern are three general categories often used to categorize feminist methodologies. See Harding (1987).
5. Positivist rules seem particularly potent in violently divided situations, where research seeks to avoid "taking up" sides. Yet in a recent Reflecting on Peace Practice Project (RPP) workshop, it was pointed out that in times of conflict, there rarely is anyone who does not have an interest, there rarely is an actor who can remain neutral.
6. Chris Corrin reflects upon anger she encountered among Kosovo women regarding Western media portrayals of women in the Balkans: "A lack of attention was paid to the international media tendencies, from 1991, to portray 'Balkan women' as older, wearing headscarves and doing physical work in the fields – that is, 'backward' within European cultures" (2001: 90).

REFERENCES

Alcoff, Linda, ed. (1998) *Epistemologies: The Big Questions*, Oxford: Blackwell.

Amnesty International (1995) *Human Rights are Women's Rights*, New York: AI USA.

Anderson, Mary (1999) *Do No Harm. How Aid can support peace – or war*, Boulder Colo.: Lynne Rienner.

Bell, Diane; Caplan, Pat; and Karim, Wzir Jhan, eds. (1993) *Gendered Fields: Women, Men and Ethnography*, London: Routledge.

Cockburn, Cynthia (1999) *The Space Between Us: Gender and Nation*, New Jersey: Zed Books.

Copelon, Emily (1995) "Gendered war crimes", in Julie Peters and Andrea Wolper, eds., *Women's Rights, Human Rights*, New York: Routledge, pp. 197–214.

Corrin, Chris (2001) "Post-conflict reconstruction and gender analysis in Kosova", *International Feminist Journal of Politics* 3(1): 78–103.

Crisp, Jeff (2000) "Thinking outside the box: evaluation and humanitarian action", *Forced Migration Review* 1(8): 4–7.

England, Kim (1994) "Getting personal: reflexivity, positionality, and feminist research", *Professional Geographer* 46(1): 80–89.

Forbes Martin, Susan (1992) *Refugee Women*, New Jersey: Zed Books.

Harding, Sandra (1987) *Feminism and Methodology, Social Science Issues*, Milton Keynes: Open University Press.

Human Rights Watch (1997) *Uncertain Refuge: Protection of the Rights of Refugee Women*, http://www.hrw.org/hrw/reports/1997/gen3/General-o4.htm.

Kirsh, Gesa E. (1999) *Ethical Dilemmas in Feminist Research: The Politics of Location*, Albany: State University of New York Press.

Marchand, Marianne H. and Parpart, Jane L., eds. (1995) *Feminism, Postmodernism, Development*, London: Routledge.

Newbury and Baldwin (2000) "Aftermath: Women's organizations in postconflict Rwanda", *Working Paper 304*, Washington, DC: USAID, Centre for Development Information and Evaluation.

Parpart, Jane L. (1995) "Deconstructing the Development 'Expert': Gender, Development and the 'Vulnerable Groups'", in Marianne H. Marchand and Jane L. Parpart, eds., *Feminism, Postmodernism, Development*, London: Routledge, pp. 221–243.

Porter, Elisabeth (2003) "Women, Political Decision-Making and Peace-building in Conflict Regions", *Global Change, Peace and Security* 15(3): 245–262.

Turner, Simon (1999) "Angry young men in camps: gender, age and class relations among Burundian refugees in Tanzania", UNHCR Working Paper No. 9, June.

Turshen, M. and Twagiramariya, C., eds. (1998), *What Women do in Wartime*, London: Zed Books.

UNESCO (1998) *African Women's Report: Post-conflict Reconstruction in Africa: A Gender Perspective Ethiopia*, Addis Ababa: UNESCO.

UNIFEM (2001) *Engendering Peace: Reflections on the Burundi Peace Process*, Kenya, Nairobi: UNIFEM.

UNHCR, UNDP, UNFPA, UNICEF, and UNIFEM (1998) *Best Practices in Peacebuilding and Non-Violent Conflict Resolution: Some Documented African Women's Peace Initiatives*, Vernier, Switzerland: UNHCR.

Uvin, Peter (2001) "Difficult choices in the new post-conflict agenda: The international community on Rwanda after the genocide", *Third World Quarterly* 22(2): 177–189.

Wolf, Diane (1996) "Situating feminist dilemmas in fieldwork", in Donald Wolf, ed., *Feminist Dilemmas in Fieldwork*, Boulder, Colo.: Westview Press.

Conclusion: Reflections on contemporary research in Africa

Elisabeth Porter

This book includes a diverse range of themes, approaches, methodologies, ethical emphases, and suggestions of ways to conduct social science research. The reader has been exposed to some of the complexities in relating methodological research theories to actual practices of ethnic conflict and violence in Africa. In conclusion, I make two final points about the commonality within all social science research and the differences that ethnic conflict makes to such research. First, there are common principles of research methodology and ethics that are relevant to all social science research methodologies. Such accepted principles are required even in the context of this book's focus on violent societies and ethnic conflict. Second, there are different principles that are specific to conducting research in divided societies and further differences that are specific to doing research on ethnic conflict in Africa. This classification is not simplistic; rather, it is important to state.

Additionally, the cultural specificity of different parts of Africa with its different ethnic conflicts amongst different cultural groups of Africans needs to be incorporated into research methodologies. "Analysis and interpretations of Africa must start with Africa. Meanings and interpretation should derive from social organization and social relations paying close attention to specific cultural and local contexts" (Oyewumi, 2002: 8). After outlining the commonalities and differences in research methods and ethics, this conclusion also briefly outlines three areas in which further research is necessary, namely, globalization, African interests, and current African imperatives.

Common principles of research

First, there are some principles of research methodology and ethics that are common to all research projects, regardless of the country, culture, community, or conflict under investigation. In particular, what is common to all research projects is the need for an appropriate methodology, the sound application of ethical procedures, and an insightful theoretical analysis to explain the research findings. It is worth summarizing these three common elements to all research projects.

First, all research projects require an appropriate methodology that is suitable to each research project, is carefully thought through and then is rigorously applied. The starting point of social science research usually is a central research question or questions, something that puzzles the researcher and prompts investigation. The methodology emerges in the search for the answers. As Marie Smyth and Gillian Robinson summarize, "*quality* research in the context of a violently divided society" includes socially relevant foci, considers complexity and polarized perspectives, collects informative data, is reliably ethical and responsible, is accountable, positions the researchers and is interdisciplinary in nature (2001: 209).

Second, part of a good methodology is the imperative to develop and maintain careful ethical procedures for each empirical research project. Moral virtues like truthfulness and honesty are important in building trust amongst the people participating in the research activities. Such procedures include maintaining the ethical integrity of the research itself and, importantly, affirming ethical respect for the individuals and social groups who are the focus of the research. Issues for consideration include the way that interviewers approach research participants, whether this is through participant observation, structured interviews, informal focus groups, or questionnaires. Research participants should be aware of the purpose of the research, provide their informed consent, be assured of confidentiality and, where possible, read quotes taken from interviews prior to publication and then have access to the published research findings.

In addition to adopting a methodology that is entirely suited to each different research project and is highly ethical in its approach, the third common principle of all research is the need to select an appropriate theoretical analysis that explains the research findings. It is not sufficient to gather data; it needs to be interpreted, explained, compared, and shown how it increases knowledge. To fulfil this task, some researchers draw not on one theory alone, but on several theoretical perspectives. For example, it is possible to combine academic literature from critical social theory with literature from democratic liberal theory, or to combine radical critiques within post-colonial thought and make some socialist feminist conclusions about race, class, gender, human rights, and power (Porter, 2003). Rather than being unsystematic, such an array of diverse theoretical perspectives can produce a fascinating analysis to explain complex research findings.

The first point in this conclusion is that common principles of social science research are applicable to all intellectually valid research. This commonality applies to all research conducted on violent societies and ethnic conflict, even though the nature of the conflict varies in significant historical, socio-economic, and political ways. Yet, the difference matters, and it is to the nature of difference that we now turn.

Different practices of research in Africa

As mentioned in the book's Introduction, the need for more thinking, talking, and writing on what it means to be doing research on ethno-conflict in Africa emerged as a pragmatic response to different practices of research in Africa. Again, the issue of commonality and difference comes to the fore. All authors in this book commonly work on, amongst other topics, African issues. However, as elaborated later, they come from different personal positionings. Also, Africa is not a homogenous continent. As we know, there are massive political differences within each nation-state with regard to the historical legacies of colonialism, the effects of post-colonialism, and conflicts about national identity. Then, there are practical differences in regions as well as states with regard to levels of economic development, education, poverty, health, HIV/AIDS and, of course, violence or stability.

Further, even within one nation-state, there are numerous cultural sensitivities to be aware of. Different rituals, myths, traditions, and tribal rivalries influence the nature of intra-state conflict. Accordingly, the research must always be attuned culturally to the particularities of each region under scrutiny. Common principles of research methodology and ethics therefore must be informed by adaptability and deep insight into the cultural specificity of different practices in different parts of Africa (Osaghae, 1999a). Further, the whole area of methodology in African research is ongoing as innovative sources and epistemological approaches continue to emerge (Falola and Jennings, 2003).

Eghosa Osaghae (2001) explains how the reinvigoration in research on ethnic conflict in Africa began in the mid-1980s. This search for new paradigms was due both to external factors like "post-Cold War realities and the global forces of democratization and market reforms" (ibid.: 15) and to internal crises of the ethnic intensification of protracted civil wars and the fragility of post-colonial states. In such contexts, there was an urgency to understand more about the devastating nature of multi-ethnic violent states. As Osaghae reminds us, "By the close of the 1990s, virtually all African States were embroiled in one form of internal war or the other" (ibid.: 21). Research findings and their recommendations can play a crucial role in understanding conflict, resolving crises, preventing civil strife, and suggesting creative strategies for non-violent intervention.

Research issues for consideration

There are three remaining reflective questions raised in this conclusion. Who does the research on ethno-conflict and violence in Africa? What is the prime focus of this research on ethno-conflict and violence in Africa? What are the contemporary African issues that social scientists need to research further? The tentative answers may surprise the reader. I explore these in relation to: first, globalization and the diaspora; second, the relationship between African studies and Africana studies; and, third, to contemporary African imperatives. However, in exploring these issues, I am very conscious of my positioning as a white Australian working in Northern Ireland who has not yet visited Africa. Thus, my reflections can only be partial, and certainly are open to debate.

Globalization and the diaspora

The first question to consider here is, "who does the research on violence and ethno-conflict in Africa"? The identity of the researcher inevitably affects the conceptualization of research, strategies used, and conclusions made. Several authors in this book are not African, but have an intense interest in African research. They write as "outsiders" like myself, or as "inside-outsiders" – that is, "working in the culture, yet outside of mainstream identities" (Porter, 2000: 164). There are many ethical and methodological issues raised by this researcher positioning with regard to the focus of attention, potential siding with one group, access to information, and acceptance within or alienation from the local community. With some scholarship, there are African scholars who no longer live in Africa, but who return to conduct fieldwork and gain first-hand knowledge of their research focus, or who maintain close ties to colleagues and various sources of information despite not being able to conduct research from an African base.

Then, there are African researchers who are living, working, and researching in an African context. It is this group of researchers who often face personal danger in their work, not only because of the risks they take in interviewing guerrilla groups, rival tribal groups, or militias, but because of their new-found possession of controversial explosive knowledge. This group have a deep appreciation of the political, policy, and legislative implications of their research. They clearly have in-depth knowledge, experience, and insight into aspects of African life.

Each of these categories of researchers – the outsider, the inside/ outsider, the African scholar working in the diaspora, and the African scholar working in Africa – offers different and valuable contributions to scholarly discourse. Clearly, unique insight is possible from the last category. What differs is who they are accountable to – Western academics, African universities, UN agencies, NGOs, private funders, humanitarian organizations, or African grassroots community groups. Also, their notions of Africa may differ.

For example, consider African researchers, working on African concerns, but who are not working in Africa. Anyone living and working away from "home" often feels pangs of alienation, sorrow, and nostalgia at being so far away from all that is familiar. Yet many researchers of all cultures have had to leave "home" for all sorts of reasons in order to write with freedom. Nunuddin Farah, the Somalian writer who has been in exile since the 1970s, is explicit: "For me, distance distils; ideas become clearer and better worth pursuing" (in Olaniyan, 2003: 1). Involuntary exile is prompted by fear of state, tribal, ethnic, or religious persecution. Yet voluntary exile also challenges the limits of the nation-state within an increasingly globalized world. Transnational social movements, globalized markets, internet technology, and travel contribute to, amongst other things, the discontent of stark material inequalities (Stiglitz, 2002), and also to "the creation of new hybrid entities, transnational phenomena like diasporic communities" (Albrow, 1997: 94). Responses to globalization and the diaspora vary. Fantu Cheru's vision of an "African renaissance" is one that embodies a "guided embrace of globalization with a commitment to resist" (2002: xv). That is, Cheru challenges African governments to address the obstacles to economic development and "renew democracy, invest in education, revitalize agricultural production, reduce poverty, strengthen regional economic cooperation, manage urbanization, and prevent conflicts" (Lavelle, 2004: 155) prior to being able to grasp any opportunity that the global economy may offer.

This relationship between globalization and the diaspora is intimate. Some may even suggest, symbiotic. Yet, Tejumola Olaniyan perceptively suggests "a conceptual shift", that: "Diaspora, with its evocation of large-scale dispersal into a boundless space, is to the age of the global what exile, with its intimation of alienation from a national homeland, is to the age of the nation-state" (Olaniyan, 2003: 2). That is, "global diaspora", seems "to recognize a world where exile is at such a pace, frequency and scale as to require redescription as 'diaspora'" (ibid.). Nigerian Nobel Laureate, Wole Soyinke, in noting the African "brain drain", another symptom of globalization, refers to being "twice bitten" (1990), with the plights of colonialism and neocolonialism. He suggests that these "bites" place a moral responsibility on researchers and writers to help heal the wounds caused by confrontations with the state that forces people into exile.

Yet, exile need not be solely physical. As the Kenyan writer, Ngugi wa Thiong'o writes, "there is a larger sense, in which we can talk of exile in African literature" (1993: 106), and he refers here to the educated elite who either went abroad or stayed in African universities, but whose "curricula reflected little or nothing of the local surroundings", and whose African universities had close partnerships "with the British ruling class" (ibid.). With such "Eurocentrism", it is inevitable that "Europe is represented as the source of knowledge and Europeans as knowers" (Oyewumi, 2002: 1). Oyeronke Oyewumi (2002: 1) writes:

The goal is to find ways in which African research can be better informed by local concerns and interpretations and at the same time, concurrently, for African experiences to be taken into account in general theory-building, the structural racism of the global system not withstanding.

The relationship between the local and the global is crucial. Tejumola Olaniyan argues that epistemological issues "about the *nature* of the postcolonial State ... are precisely the fundamental issues the social sciences avoided ... and only now discreetly addressing" (2003: 3). Yet understandably, he is disturbed by the degree to which the politics of a global diaspora should be embraced, given that "globality and the global diaspora seem to be an unequal and one-way traffic" (ibid.: 4). Olaniyan calls on Rey Chow's sobering reminder of what it means to be "stuck at home" (1993: 118) and that researchers working outside of their own national boundaries, often "forget the difference between one's experiences as a diasporic intellectual and that of those 'stuck at home'" (Olaniyan, 2003: 4). Certainly, the relationship of African intellectuals to the Pan African project, the state, nationalism, and societies wracked by violence is complex (see Mkandawire, 2005).

I began this section by asking which researchers are working on ethno-conflict and violence in Africa, and the answer is various. African researchers, non-African researchers, and diasporic global African communities enrich the body of intellectual research.

Relationship between African studies and Africana studies

The second question to consider is, "what is the prime focus of this research on ethno-conflict and violence in Africa?" One response to this question is offered by Oyekan Owomoyeka who writes:

Perhaps the surest way of getting Africa back into African Studies is to get African Studies back to Africa ... But, even if we cannot return African Studies to Africa in geographical terms, we could do so at least epistemologically and paradigmatically (1994: 96–97).

As Kwasi Konadu reflects, "Owomoyeka's statement is principally a conceptual claim premised on the anchoring and ownership of the study of Africa(ns) by Africans" (2004: 33). Konadu is making the point that if research on Africa is driven by methodological paradigms that have been established by non-African researchers, one needs to ask whose interests are being served. He is affirming the significance of Owomoyeka's problem for the study of Africa(ns), by which Konadu means "an African centred approach that conceptualizes reality and situates Africans within their cosmological, symbolic, and pragmatic universe" (2004: 34). This explicit methodological approach "affirms African agency" (ibid.) as the important prime focus of research in Africa.

Konadu is making a distinction here between the academic study of Africa, that is, African studies, dominated by "non-Africans studying Africa from Africans studying themselves and the world they exist in" (2004: 34). When European or American academia provide the categories for social science research of non-Western cultures, differences and cultural specificity sometimes are problematized unwittingly and seen as extraordinary, rather than as methodologically significant. Konadu's claim is that it is Africana studies that have brought about a challenging construction of knowledge with its motto of "commitment, connectedness, and consciousness" (ibid.: 35). Africana studies build on the global African community in order to develop research methods, epistemological concerns, and theoretical constructs that are located conceptually and culturally in Africa.

The section above addressed the relevance of the global to research methodologies. In this section, I have discussed the need for research to be firmly grounded in local cultural concerns that really assist the empowering of Africans. Thus, in terms of the focus of this book, research on violence, divided societies, and ethno-conflict in Africa should contribute positively to the lives of African people, and to peace and conflict studies generally. The vision of these studies is of a world where communities are not torn apart by ethnic tensions, rivalries, and violence. The great hope is that research on ethno-conflict and violence in Africa will eventually affirm and empower all those who are working to realize this vision of peace with justice.

African research imperatives

The third question to reflect on is, "What are the contemporary African issues that social scientists need to research further in order to assist the vision of a world where there is an appreciation of ethnic diversity, rather than violent struggle over ethnic conflict?" Many issues have already arisen in this book. There are recurring themes in all its chapters relating to the patterns of ethnic tensions and conflict, the harm of civil war and violence, the debilitating effects of civil strife, the crippling nature of poverty, the disempowering consequences of colonialism, and the ambiguous role of the nation-state in a globalizing world. Certainly, there remain real contradictions in the desire to affirm national African identity (Nobles, 1998), which is an important part of affirming moral agency, and the propensity for extreme ethnic consciousness to be used ideologically to justify immoral political decisions of an authoritarian, non-democratic nature, that lead so frequently to violent conflicts (Osaghae, 1999b). These contradictions need to be teased out further, not for the sake of intellectual posturing, but that a greater understanding of what prompts conflict may assist the prevention of subsequent conflict or the resolution of a new conflict when it does arise, or inform early warning intervention strategies that minimize the eruption of violence.

Whilst research for knowledge's sake is necessary, it is ethically difficult to justify the acquisition of knowledge for knowledge's sake in situations where lives are being lost ... Improved knowledge about violent societies may not necessarily result in improved responses to the division and violence, yet the desire for such improvement is a motivator for much of the research that is carried out (Smyth, 2001: 3–4).

There clearly are a host of pressing socio-economic issues that often are the prime triggers to violent conflict, particularly relating to economic inequality, poverty, illiteracy, women's subordination, the exploitation of communities by global multinational companies, and the Global North's culpability in providing easy access to small arms. Then, there are the terrible human pains that emerge as a direct consequence of violent ethnic conflict in Africa such as deaths, the guilt at being alive, war-rape, contracting HIV and then AIDS, children fathered by rival ethnic groups, the rise in children-headed households, refugees, displaced persons, memory flashbacks, emotional trauma, disruption to communities, and an incredible sense of haunting loss. The answer to the final question as to where further research should be concentrated must surely lie in three areas of research that are most likely to lead to: first, *the empowering of African people*; second, *the building of human capacities* that allow people to flourish; and, third, *the realization of a just peace* where research on violent conflict ceases to be necessary. Ultimately, greater attention to indigenous knowledge of ethnic conflict and creation of indigenous research strategies lies in the capable hands of African researchers.

REFERENCES

Albrow, Martin (1997) *The Global Age: State and Society Beyond Modernity*, Stanford: Stanford University Press.

Cheru, Fantu (2002) *African Renaissance: Roadmaps to the Challenge of Globalization*, London/New York: Zed Books.

Chow, Rey (1993) *Writing Diaspora: Tactics of Intervention in Contemporary Cultural Studies*, New York: St. Martin's Press.

Falola, Toyin and Jennings, Christian, eds. (2003) *Sources and Methods in African History. Spoken, Written, Unearthed*, Rochester, NY: University of Rochester Press.

Konadu, Kwasi (2004) "The cultural identity of Africa and the global tasks of Africana studies", *African Studies Quarterly* 7(4): 33–40.

Lavelle, Kathryn (2004) "Review of Fantu Cheru's African Renaissance: Roadmaps to the challenge of globalization", *Journal of Modern African Studies* 42(1): 155–162.

Mkandawire, Thandika, ed. (2005) *African Intellectuals. Rethinking Politics, Language, Gender and Development*, London: Zed Books.

Ngugi wa Thiong'o (1993) *Moving the Centre: The Struggle for Cultural Freedoms*, London: James Currey.

Nobles, Wade (1998) "To be African or Not to be: The question of identity or authenticity – some preliminary thought", in Reginald L. Jones, ed., *African American Identity Development*, Hampton, VA: Cobb and Henry, pp. 187–192.

Olaniyan, Tejumola (2003) "African writers, exile, and the politics of a global Diaspora", *West Africa Review* 4(1): 1–5, www.westafricareview.com/war/, accessed, 12.10.04.

Osaghae, Eghosa, E. (1999a) "Conflict research in Africa", *International Journal on World Peace* XVI(4): 53–64.

——— (1999b) "Democratization in Sub-Saharan Africa: Faltering prospects, new hopes", *Journal of Contemporary African Studies* 17(1): 5–28.

——— (2001) "The role and function of research in divided societies: the case of Africa", in Marie Smyth and Gillian Robinson, eds., *Researching Violently Divided Societies. Ethical and Methodological Issues*, Tokyo: United Nations University Press/London: Pluto Press, pp. 12–33.

Owomoyeka, Oyekan (1994) "With friends like these ... a critique of pervasive Anti-Africanisms in current African studies, epistemology and methodology", *African Studies Review* 37(3): 77–101.

Oyewumi, Oyeronke (2002) "Conceptualizing gender: The Eurocentric foundations of feminist concepts and the challenge of African epistemologies", *Jenda: A Journal of Culture and African Women Studies* 2(1): 1–9.

Porter, Elisabeth (2000) "Risks and responsibilities: creating dialogical spaces in Northern Ireland", *International Feminist Journal of Politics* 2(2): 163–184.

———— (2003) "Women, political decision-making, and peace-building", *Global Change, Peace and Security* 15(3): 245–262.

Smyth, Marie (2001) "Introduction", in Marie Smyth and Gillian Robinson, eds., *Researching Violently Divided Societies. Ethical and Methodological Issues*, Tokyo: United Nations University Press/London: Pluto Press, pp. 1–11.

Smyth, Marie and Robinson, Gillian (2001) "Conclusions", in Marie Smyth and Gillian Robinson, eds., *Researching Violently Divided Societies. Ethical and Methodological Issues*, Tokyo: United Nations University Press/London: Pluto Press, pp. 207–209.

Soyinka, Wole (1990) "Twice bitten: The fate of Africa's culture producers", *PMLA* 105(1): 110–120.

Stiglitz, Joseph (2002) *Globalization and its Discontents*, New York: W. W. Norton.

Index

166